ESSENTIALS

of the

FAITH

UPDATED

∽

Our Sunday Visitor books by Father McBride

Celebrating the Mass
The Millennium
Veritatis Splendor
Guides to the *Catechism of the Catholic Church:*
- *Essentials of the Faith, Updated*
- *Father McBride's College Catechism*
- *Father McBride's Family Catechism*
- *Father McBride's Teen Catechism*

Our Sunday Visitor's Popular Bible Study:
- *The Kingdom and the Glory* (Commentary on Matthew's Gospel)
- *To Love and Be Loved by Jesus* (Commentary on Mark's Gospel)
- *The Human Face of Jesus* (Commentary on Luke's Gospel)
- *The Divine Presence of Jesus* (Commentary on John's Gospel)
- *The Gospel of the Holy Spirit* (Commentary on the Acts of the Apostles)
- *The Second Coming of Jesus* (Commentary on the Book of Revelation)

ESSENTIALS
of the
FAITH
UPDATED

A Guide to the
CATECHISM
of the Catholic Church

ALFRED McBRIDE, O.PRAEM.

Our Sunday Visitor Publishing Division
Our Sunday Visitor, Inc.
Huntington, Indiana 46750

Nihil Obstat:
Rev. Msgr. Francis D. Kelly, S.T.L., Ph.D.

Imprimatur:
✠ Bernard Cardinal Law
Archbishop of Boston
February 4, 1994

The *nihil obstat* and *imprimatur* are official declarations that a book or pamphlet is free of doctrinal or moral error. No implication is contained therein that those who have granted the *nihil obstat* and the *imprimatur* agree with the content, opinions or statements expressed.

Acknowledgments

I wish to acknowledge the tremendous support and sponsorship given to this project by Father John Bradley and Robert Gallagher of Good Will Publishers of Charlotte, North Carolina, as well as Robert Lockwood and Greg Erlandson of Our Sunday Visitor Publishers of Huntington, Indiana.

Material for the Focus sections of this book has been gleaned from many sources. The quotations taken from ancient and well-known persons in the Catholic Church have been noted throughout the text. For the translations of many of these, we would like to thank the International Commission on English in the Liturgy.

Contemporary citations are taken from the following:

- *People of the Lie: The Hope for Healing Human Evil*, M. Scott Peck
- *The People's Religion*, George Gallup, Jr., and Jim Castelli
- *Your God Is Too Small*, J. B. Phillips
- *The Catholic Vision*, Edward O'Connor, C.S.C.
- *Life of Christ* and *Three to Get Married*, Archbishop Fulton J. Sheen
- *Journeys to Glory*, Marjorie Young and Adam Bujak
- *Poems That Touch the Heart*, A. L. Alexander (editor)
- *The Splendor of the Church*, Henri De Lubac, S.J.
- *Fundamentals of the Faith*, Peter Kreeft
- *Mary, Mother of the Lord*, Karl Rahner, S.J.
- *Newman: On Being a Christian*, Ian Ker
- *The 7 Habits of Highly Effective People*, Stephen R. Covey
- *Small Is Beautiful: Economics as if People Mattered*, E. F. Schumacher
- *Why Johnny Can't Tell Right from Wrong*, William Kilpatrick
- *Pope John XXIII*, Peter Hebblethwaite
- *Mary for Today*, Hans Urs von Balthasar
- *The Faith of Millions*, John A. O'Brien
- *John Paul II in America*, Pope John Paul II
- *Vatican Council II: Conciliar and Post Conciliar Documents*, Austin Flannery, O.P., Gen. Ed.

Bibliographic information for these books can be found beginning on page 206.

Those quotations not attributed are written by the author.

Table of Contents

Preface

On October 11, 1992, Pope John Paul II published his Apostolic Constitution *Depositum Fidei*, introducing the *Catechism of the Catholic Church*. He chose a publication date that marked the thirtieth anniversary of the opening of Vatican II.

In this document, he writes, "I declare it [the *Catechism*] to be a sure norm for teaching the faith. . . . Therefore, I ask the Church's pastors and the Christian faithful to receive this *Catechism* in a spirit of communion and to use it assiduously in fulfilling their mission of proclaiming the faith and calling people to the Gospel life."

This exhortation reflects the epistle to Timothy, which stresses the need to serve the deposit of faith with loving care. "O Timothy, guard what has been entrusted to you. . . . Guard this rich trust with the help of the Holy Spirit that dwells within us" (1 Tm 6:20; 2 Tm 1:14).

Such also was the vision of Pope John XXIII when he asked the Fathers of Vatican II both to guard and to present better the heritages of our faith. Why? To make the Gospel more accessible to the Christian faithful and to all people of good will. Hence the council did not concentrate on condemning the errors of our time, but rather strove calmly to demonstrate the power and beauty of Christian doctrine.

This same positive spirit pervades the *Catechism*. It contains the inherent beauty and intrinsic attractiveness of the teachings of Christ that appeal to the mind and heart. Pope Paul VI said that the full presentation of these teachings must be at the heart of evangelization. "There is no true evangelization if the name, the teaching, the life, the promises, the kingdom and the mystery of Jesus of Nazareth, the Son of God, are not proclaimed" (On Evangelization, 22).

The *Catechism of the Catholic Church* contains this hidden energy of the Good News and will be more effective when all of us absorb its spirit and content. Convinced people convince others. When we embark on a lifelong journey of faith conversion, our faith conviction will affect others. Converted teachers convert students by the grace of the Holy Spirit working both in the witnessing teacher and the listening student.

Our Holy Father goes on to say, "This *Catechism* is given that it may be a sure and authentic reference text for teaching Catholic doctrine and particularly for preparing local catechisms."

In this book, *Essentials of the Faith*, Norbertine Father Alfred McBride ably implements this guideline of the Holy Father. He makes the core wealth of the *Catechism* available to all Catholics, while at the same time stimulating their interest in reading and studying the *Catechism of the Catholic Church* on their own.

The positive tone of Father McBride's book echoes the nonpolemical character of the *Catechism*. Our Church rightly rejoices in a theology of abundance, which gives her every reason to be hope-filled. St. Paul refers to this when he says, "To me, the very least of all the holy ones, this grace was given, to preach to the Gentiles the inscrutable riches of Christ. . . . Oh, the depth of the riches and wisdom and knowledge of God" (Eph 4:8; Rom 11:33).

One of the practical outcomes of the *Catechism* should be a religious literacy which will enable Catholics to know, explain, apply, and defend their faith. Numerous studies have identified this need. Our Holy Father specifies this as a goal of the *Catechism*: "It is offered to all the faithful who wish to deepen their knowledge of the unfathomable riches of salvation. The *Catechism of the Catholic Church* is offered to every individual who asks us to give an account of the hope that is in us (cf. 1 Pt 3:15) and who wants to know what the Catholic Church teaches." The glossary of terms found in each chapter of Father McBride's book implements the *Catechism*'s goal of religious literacy.

Finally, the *Catechism* is meant to stir up the faith of the reader. In *Essentials of the Faith*, you will find a prayer and focus meditation in each lesson, thus providing a practical application of the *Catechism*'s intention to integrate the truths of faith with prayer and reflection.

I am pleased to recommend Father McBride's *Essentials of the Faith*. May it inspire its readers to turn to the *Catechism* itself, where they will find the theology of abundance to which the author points.

✠ Bernard Cardinal Law
Archbishop of Boston
January 1994

Introduction

> I rarely preach a sermon, but I go to this beautiful and complete catechism to get both my matter and my doctrine.
>
> Cardinal Newman, *Apologia*

In the above quote, John Henry Cardinal Newman was referring to the *Roman Catechism* commissioned by the Council of Trent in 1546. One of the greatest accomplishments of Trent was the survival and use of this *Roman Catechism* for four centuries. There were 817 editions in 17 languages from 1566 to 1978. Pope John XXIII still recommended its use in 1960.

Today, another catechism claims our attention. On June 25, 1992, Pope John Paul II officially approved the new *Catechism of the Catholic Church*, the first such complete expression of the Church's catechetical mission since the sixteenth century!

In the introductory section of this book, I will treat of the *Roman Catechism* of 1566, *the Baltimore Catechism* of 1885, and the genesis and purpose of the new *Catechism*.

First, I should define the use of the word *catechism*. Most people correctly identify a catechism with a question-and-answer book that communicates the basic teachings of the Catholic Church in a systematic and comprehensive way. Luther originated this type of catechism.

The second and less known definition of a catechism is that of an extended exposition, in essay form, of basic Catholic teachings — also in a systematic and comprehensive manner. The Church has published only two such catechisms: the *Roman Catechism* of Trent and the newly published *Catechism of the Catholic Church*.

The *Roman Catechism*

The word *catechism* comes from a Greek term that means to speak so as to be heard. The term also means "to echo." All cultures up to the invention of the printing press in Mainz in 1450 were oral societies. A catechist would speak a teaching of the Church and instruct the listener to "echo" it, to repeat it until it was learned by heart.

Martin Luther brilliantly employed the new technology of the printing press in the publication of his catechism in 1529, thirty-seven long years before Catholics caught on to the idea. He changed the old oral idea of the "speak and echo" method into the "question and answer" one, and fixed it in print.

Twenty-five years after Luther's break with the Church, Pope Paul III convened the Council of Trent. The sessions of the council would last, with extended breaks, for twenty-one years. In 1546, the bishops at Trent made their first hesitant attempt to develop a Catholic catechism. However, some of the bishops believed that a book of homilies for the parish clergy might be a better idea. One year later the bishops returned to the proposal to do a catechism.

Not until 1562 did the issue come up again when the emperor Ferdinand instructed his bishop-delegates to urge the council Fathers to create a catechism. Similar requests poured in from the other Catholic kings and princes of Europe.

In 1563, a committee of bishops and theologians seriously undertook the production of a catechism. They did not finish the task. The council ended and passed the responsibility for completing the catechism to Pope Pius IV. He appointed his nephew, Cardinal Charles Borromeo of Milan, to supervise the work of yet another catechism committee. They labored on but did not complete the work by the death of Pius IV.

The next Pope, St. Pius V, ascetic, strong-willed, and determined, forcefully implemented the decrees of Trent and completed the *Roman Catechism*. He published it in 1566. The *Roman Catechism* was addressed to parish priests: Neither Catholics nor Protestants in this period stressed the teaching role of parents, as is the case today.

Divided into four parts, the *Roman Catechism* discussed the Creed, Sacraments, Commandments, and the Our Father. The sequence reflected the view that God's gracious salvation enunciated in the creed and received in the sacraments should be responded to by Christian witness in keeping the commandments and strengthened by a life of prayer. Joseph Cardinal Ratzinger praised this ordering of catechesis in his 1983 speech on catechetics in Lyons. The new *Catechism of the Catholic Church* follows the same order.

The *Roman Catechism* was not polemical. It was non-controversial. It aimed to present Catholic truths and their inherent attractiveness, rather than to refute the errors of the times. It became the enduring sourcebook for subsequent catechesis up to its last edition in 1978.

What was actually used to teach religion after Trent? Parish priests frequently used the *Roman Catechism* to prepare their sermons. But for teaching religion to young people at various levels, St. Peter Canisius (1521-1597) in Germany and St. Robert Bellarmine (1542-1621) in Italy wrote question-and-answer catechisms in imitation of Luther's method. They based the content on the *Roman Catechism*.

Both authors were incredibly successful. Canisius published a catechism in 1566. It had 223 questions and answers. In his own lifetime, it went through 200 editions and was translated widely. In nineteenth-century Germany, Canisius and catechism were synonymous.

Bellarmine published a short catechism in 1597. For the next three centuries, his catechism was the most widely translated Catholic religion book after the Bible and Thomas à Kempis's (1380-1471) *Imitation of Christ*.

The *Catechism of the Catholic Church*

At the Synod of Bishops in 1985, Boston's Bernard Cardinal Law addressed the assembly with these words: "I propose a commission of cardinals to prepare a draft of a conciliar catechism to be promulgated by the Holy Father after consulting the bishops of the world." Many bishops concurred with him.

Pope John Paul II also agreed and announced the writing of a new catechism on June 28, 1986. Four years later, in November 1990, a consultation draft of the *Catechism* (in English, French, and Spanish) was sent to bishops around the world. The bishops were given six months to examine it and send back recommendations.

Bishop Christoph Von Schönborn, auxiliary bishop of Vienna, chaired the catechism committee of seven bishop-editors and a specialist on the Eastern Churches. With the help of a computer, the editors examined the 1,000 replies and 24,000 recommendations for the consultation draft. They amended the text in the light of the consultation. The world's bishops were overwhelmingly favorable (90 percent) about the draft.

What does this new *Catechism* contain?

It is built on four pillars:

(1) Creed — The Faith Professed

(2) Sacraments — The Faith Celebrated

(3) Commandments — The Faith Lived

(4) Our Father — The Faith Prayed

Part One: Creed — The Faith Professed

This is a revelation-based catechesis. The first section on the creed outlines the revelation of God — Father, Son, and Spirit — in the creation of the world and the salvation of all peoples. The Father accomplished his divine plan through the Incarnation, life, death, and Resurrection of his Son, Jesus Christ. By the action of the Holy Spirit this is realized in the life of the Church. This is the faith that Catholics profess.

The creed emphasizes the acts of the Holy Trinity made visible in sacred history, enshrined in the Bible, and proclaimed by the Church. The dynamic is a dialogue of salvation between God and believers. The Holy

Trinity has revealed the divine plan of salvation. The human response occurs in the faith of believers inspired by the loving action of the Holy Spirit. This is the vision for understanding the creed.

Part Two: Sacraments — The Faith Celebrated

The second section on the sacraments portrays them as the continuation of the divine plan in the life of the Church. The mighty deeds of grace performed by the Father in the first covenant were perfectly realized in the ministry and new covenant of Jesus Christ, the Word made flesh. Now, under the action of the Holy Spirit, believers in every age can experience the saving power of Christ's life, death, and Resurrection by celebrating the sacraments in a faith-filled and active way.

In each sacramental celebration, the Spirit opens the minds and hearts of believers to receive Christ's graces of salvation and spiritual renewal. Once again the dialogue of salvation is at work. Each sacrament is an occasion in which Jesus offers us the treasures of divine love. Each sacrament is an opportunity for us to respond with faith to that presentation of God's gracious love.

Part Three: Commandments — The Faith Lived

The third section on the commandments concerns the divine plan of salvation as it is lived in the daily affairs of believers. The Christian goes forth into the world armed with the creed as a narrative of divine love and the sacraments as the celebratory events in which the love of Jesus Christ is experienced. Empowered by faith in what the creed proclaims, what the sacraments accomplish, and guided by the Church, the believer witnesses Christian individual and social morality. How? By following Christ's two great commandments of love of God and loving others as we love ourselves and observing the Ten Commandments in the light of Christ's laws of love.

The sections on the creed and sacraments unfold the great teachings and experience of a loving covenant between the Trinity and the Christian. Now, the Holy Spirit enables the Christian to respond by living Christ's laws of love and the Ten Commandments. Covenant fulfills Christ's dream of how and why commandments should be kept. The commandments are acts of love that respond to the gracious gift of salvation received from Jesus. They are more than legal rules. They are ways of saying to Jesus, "I love you."

Part Four: Our Father — The Faith Prayed

The fourth section is on the Our Father and the role of prayer in Christian life. Creed and sacraments illustrate how the Trinity offers us divine love. Beatitudes and commandments show us how to live that love in daily life. Prayer is the indispensable means of staying in love with God. By covenant we fall in love with God. By prayer we stay in love with God.

In prayer, the Holy Spirit cleanses us of lack of love and fills us with divine affection. In prayer we acquire the inner energy to live up to our Christian commitment. Prayer is the internal power that makes creed, sacraments, and commandments vividly alive for us.

This is the splendid master plan of the *Catechism of the Catholic Church*. It draws us to identify with Jesus Christ and the inner life of the Church, which is Christ's Body. It is above all a profoundly spiritual text, and its purpose is our spiritual renewal.

> This book we pray will bring us love
> And lead us to our home above
> Where we shall with our voices raise
> A hymn of everlasting praise.

The *Baltimore Catechism*

For millions of Catholics in the United States, the word *catechism* means the *Baltimore Catechism*. It also brings back memories of memorized questions and answers, the method used for centuries to impart a basic knowledge of the teachings of Jesus Christ as given to us by the Church. That method, first introduced by Luther, was adopted by both Protestants and Catholics (with some modifications) all the way up to the twentieth century.

What, briefly, is the history of *the Baltimore Catechism*?

Numerous catechisms in the question-and-answer format were published after the promulgation of the *Roman Catechism* in 1566. Two of them specifically influenced the *Baltimore Catechism*. First was "The Sincere Christian," the catechism of Bishop George Hay of Edinburgh, published in 1781. Archbishop John Carroll abridged Hay's catechetical writings, many of whose texts appeared in the *Baltimore Catechism*.

In Ireland, Archbishop James Butler of Cashel produced a catechism in 1775. The Synod of Maynooth revised it in 1875. Substantial portions of this edition appeared in the *Baltimore Catechism*.

At the Third Plenary Council of Baltimore in 1884, the bishops of the United States published a national catechism for our country. It was composed by J. de Consilio, a priest of Newark, New Jersey, and John Lancaster Spalding, Bishop of Peoria, Illinois.

Its 72 pages contained 421 questions and answers in 37 chapters. Its order was: Creed, Sacraments, Prayer, Commandments, and Last Things. Its publication coincided with the bishops' urging every parish to have a

Catholic school. Supporting this policy was the arrival in America of dozens of new religious congregations devoted to the teaching ministry.

The *Baltimore Catechism* served the need to have unity of faith teaching and understanding for millions of immigrant Catholics who crowded American cities, towns, and farms. Its impact was felt right up to the dawn of Vatican II in 1962. What brought about the gradual development of other ways to teach religion to our students?

We can assign the causes to the emergence of new teaching methods based on the psychological development of the students and the growth of biblical and liturgical studies.

Psychological development. All through the early twentieth century extensive research was done on how children learn and their readiness for a given body of teaching. Scholars tracked their receptivity to knowledge at given stages and the development of their reasoning skills.

As this research entered the catechetical mainstream, writers of textbooks and teachers of the materials adapted their approach to the readiness of the students. It was argued that the memorized question-and-answer method in a "one size fits all" was inadequate to the needs of the students. This method was too fixed on memory alone. There should be a broader approach that addressed the intuitive, imaginative, and reasoning capacities of students. Teachers should go beyond "What does the Church teach?" to "What does the Church mean by her teaching?" The method also emphasized using the human experiences of the students to help them understand the truths of divine revelation.

Growth of biblical and liturgical studies. The explosion of new interest in the Bible and the liturgy as sources of our spiritual growth affected the teaching of religion. This led teachers to incorporate the Bible and liturgy into catechetical lessons.

In the 1950s, Jesuit Father Johannes Hofinger proposed what he called the "Kerygmatic Method" (or, salvation history) catechesis. *Kerygma* means joyful proclamation. Of what? Of the Good News of salvation.

Hofinger based his concept on the way the apostles and Fathers of the Church taught religion. They presented the Bible as the record of God's mighty deeds of love for us and our call to respond to that graciousness with faith and love.

This Bible-based catechesis was intimately connected to Word and sacrament in the celebration of the liturgy. Behind it was this unifying principle: God the Father entered history with redeeming covenant acts of love for Israel. The prophets reinterpreted that love for successive generations and foresaw a Messiah. This covenant and prophetic promise was perfectly realized in the Incarnation, life, death, and Resurrection of the Word made flesh, Jesus Christ. It continues in the Spirit-guided life of the Church and the sacraments. All through this process, God calls us to a living, active, and conscious faith response.

What impact did this have on the content of catechesis? It caused the content to become biblical, historical, and interpersonal. Faith about God was expressed in more vivid, concrete, salvation-historical, and interpersonal language. Just like the *Baltimore Catechism*, it was based on God's revelation.

How did it work? Theoretically, the developmental, psychological method was basically a good idea. The same was true of a biblical/liturgical-based catechesis. Unfortunately, the writers and teachers often did not know how to communicate a systematic and comprehensive knowledge and understanding of basic Catholic teachings in this new context. Numerous reasons account for this: lack of scriptural knowledge, inability to translate basic teachings into a biblical/liturgical language, a tendency to substitute psychology for religion, etc.

The result has been well-documented, widespread religious illiteracy. *Baltimore Catechism* alumni knew their religion, but may not have understood it. In the new catechetics, people are willing to understand, but need something to ponder.

That is the reason why the Pope and bishops have commissioned the new *Catechism of the Catholic Church.*

How to Use the New *Catechism*

The publication of the new *Catechism of the Catholic Church* comes at an opportune time for American Catholics. The Catholic parents of the baby-boom generation have come of age. They are participating in a revival of religion in our country.

"Above all, however, the return to religion is fueled by the boomers' experiences of becoming parents – and the realization that children need a place where they can learn solid values. . . .

"It turns out that the Forever Young generation did not escape the life cycle. Like their parents before them – verily, like generations before them – as people wed, aged, became fruitful and multiplied, they turned their attentions to matters of the spirit" (*Newsweek*, December 17, 1990).

At the same time studies show that religious illiteracy is widespread. Gallup Poll surveys show that two-thirds of Catholics do not know the correct meaning of the Holy Eucharist, nor that Jesus delivered the Sermon on the Mount and composed the Our Father. The new *Catechism* is a providential response to the awakened religious spirit of today's parents and to the need for a return to religious literacy. To whom is the *Catechism* addressed, and what are its uses?

The new *Catechism of the Catholic Church* is written in essay form like its great predecessor, the *Roman Catechism* of 1566. It is addressed to the bishops of the world and to all who assist them in teaching the Catholic religion. Its purpose is our spiritual renewal through a clear, systematic, and comprehensive presentation of the essentials of Catholic faith.

In his address to the U.S. bishops of the Midwest on June 5, 1993, Pope John Paul said, "I pray that the Church in the United States will recognize in the *Catechism* . . . a basic text for the upper grades of Catholic high schools, colleges, and universities" (*Origins*, July 15, 1993). Each part of the Church will have to adapt it to its particular culture.

It is the principal sourcebook for present and future composition of religion textbooks and other teaching materials, a vision of catechesis itself, and a guide for the religiously perplexed in confusing times.

• Who, then, is expected to use this book?

Anyone involved in finding ways of sharing our Catholic faith with others. This involves: bishops and the pastoral clergy; parents; publishers and writers of religion texts; creators of media presentations; diocesan and parish leaders of religious education; volunteer and professional religion teachers; members of departments of religion in Catholic schools, colleges, and universities; and other Catholics interested in a solid and comprehensive presentation of Catholic faith.

• What is the best teaching method for using it?

This *Catechism* contains no recommendations for any particular teaching method. However, all publishers, writers, and teachers should remember this is a revelation-based catechesis. The focus is on the Father's saving action in history through his Son, Jesus Christ, and continued by the Holy Spirit through the Church and the sacraments. The human response is grace-filled faith. This interaction is a dialogue of salvation between God and humans.

A great variety of methods are suitable for communicating the faith in textbooks and materials guided by this *Catechism*. These would include:

(1) A scope and sequence of materials spread out over the primary, intermediate, junior high, and secondary levels, adapted to the mentality and readiness of the students;

(2) The use of enrichment materials from the Bible, liturgy, Church history, the lives of the saints, the witness of outstanding believers, the writ-

ings of saints and other spiritual authors, appropriate examples from the background and culture of the students;

(3) The use of all the learning faculties of the students: reason, intuition, imagination, logic, and memory;

(4) The use of the human experience of the students to involve them in the catechetical teaching under consideration. This method begins where the students are and brings them to where they ought to be. It starts with what they know to bring them to what they do not know. It assumes that the goal and focus of this effort is spiritual growth by knowing Jesus Christ personally and acquiring a knowledge of his message – becoming Catholics who are religiously literate and capable of sharing their faith;

(5) The use of a broad range of new techniques for adult education. Catechesis should not stop with the young, but be a lifelong pursuit of every Catholic adult.

• How does the *Catechism* face different cultures?

The *Catechism* advises each part of the Church to adapt its contents to the local culture. In the United States this means we will have to develop alternative approaches for the prevalent American culture as well as for the specific ethnic and cultural needs of Native Americans, Hispanic Americans, Afro-Americans, Asian Americans, and Caribbean Americans. Church history has proven that the Body of Christ has been inculturated into societies as varied as the Middle East, Greece, Rome, and Europe. It's been done before and can be done again.

Clearly then, the new *Catechism* has a wide range of methods to choose from. They will work best when the teachers remain faithful to the intention of the *Catechism* to promote faith as a relationship with Jesus Christ and faith in his message which commits us to his Church, Sacraments, Commandments, and Prayer.

Conclusion

With this, we complete our introductory material on the new *Catechism*. In the remainder of this book, I will take the lessons of the new *Catechism* and present them in a condensed and popular format. As I unfold its rich and inspiring teachings, I trust they will minister to the growth of your inner life and your commitment to Jesus Christ and his Church.

Part One

Creed: The Faith Professed

Chapter 1

Our Capacity for God

The desire for God is written in the human heart, because man is created by God and for God. . . .

Catechism, 27

Who am I? What am I doing here? Who are you? What are you doing here? At some time in everyone's life, these questions about purpose and meaning arise. Crisis, illness, tragedy, and death often provoke such questions.

If I look within my mind and heart I sense my limits. I also notice I want to reach for the unreachable stars. I have a capacity for the infinite. I have a place within me that could be a shrine for the divine, a sanctuary for the Holy One.

The atheist tells me that my outreach is a useless passion; my inner shrine will always be empty. The agnostic warns me there is no way to *know* if anyone can dwell there. The contemporary, secular humanist urges me to forget the whole quest: I should not bother to pursue my capacity for God. Do not reach for the star.

But my boundless hope presses me to summon the Holy One to come, and it urges me to seek him out. "As the hind longs for the running waters, / so my soul longs for you, O God" (Ps 42:1). When this meeting occurs, I will experience it as a miracle, a mystery, a grace. Even when I expect God to come to me, I will still experience this as a childlike surprise when it happens.

My Reason Pushes Me Toward God

Our Church asks me to notice how my reason drives me toward knowing God. This inner compulsion is not a self-deception because God has planted signs of his presence in *nature* and in my *conscience*. What I look for I can find. When the Psalmist said, "The heavens declare the glory of God" (19:1), he taught me that I can know God through the beauty of creation.

The First Vatican Council repeated this teaching: "The Church teaches that God can be known with certainty by reason from created things" (Vatican I, 3004). That Council assures me of the possibility of knowing God by reason. But it also insists that I can know God by divine Revelation. Nature tells me there is a God. Revelation tells me there is a God who loves me.

Revelation Helps Reason

Even though I can know God through reason's reflection on the universe, I seldom practice such reflection because passions darken my mind. Reason urges me to know God. Sin pulls me away from this possibility. Revelation makes reason's task easier. Because of Revelation, reason's quest for God "in the present condition of the human race can be known by all with ease" (Vatican I, 3005).

How does Revelation make reason's efforts easier?

First, by overcoming the darkness of ignorance caused by original sin. Second, by putting the backbone of certainty into an otherwise hesitant and tentative reason. Lastly, by giving me real knowledge of God free from error. It liberates me from ideas of God that mingle the true and the false together.

Revelation reminds me that my Catholic faith teaches me that I can know God without faith, though knowing God with faith is obviously better and more enriching. Such faith brings me to praise God for the signs of his existence in creation and to love God for the gift of divine Revelation that makes my search easier.

Reflection

1. *Why did God create me?*

   "Man is made to live in communion with God in whom he finds happiness" (*Catechism*, 45).

2. *How can I know God exists?*

   "When he listens to the message of creation and to the voice of conscience, man can arrive at certainty about the existence of God, the cause and the end of everything" (*Catechism*, 46).

3. *Can my reason know God?*

   "The Church teaches that the one true God, our Creator and Lord, can be known with certainty from his works, by the natural light of human reason" (*Catechism*, 47).

Prayer

Loving God, I praise you for the gift of divine Revelation which helps my reason discover you in creation and in my conscience. Thank you for giving me a capacity for your presence within the depths of my heart.

Resource

Catechism, 27-49

Glossary

Agnostic. One who claims it is impossible to know whether God exists.

Atheist. One who denies existence of God.

Revelation. God's self-disclosure of his inner life and his plan for our salvation. This Revelation is found in Scripture and Tradition.

Vatican I. A Council of the Church held in 1870.

Life Application

1. What clues are there that my mind keeps looking for truth and meaning? Is my curiosity about the world and God alive and well? Do I keep up my reading of books and articles as evidence of this?

2. Am I too "grown up" now to experience awe and wonder, or am I open to spiritual realities? In what ways? Do I sense a spiritual restlessness in my soul? What have I done lately that makes me aware of my need for God and my desire to get in touch with Christ?

3. What am I most passionate about in life? Where do I place my enthusiasms? What do I think about my answers?

Focus

The Christian says: Creatures are not born with desires unless satisfaction for those desires exists. A baby feels hunger: well, there is such a thing as food. A duckling wants to swim: well, there is such a thing as water. Men feel sexual desire: well, there is such a thing as sex. If I find in myself a desire which no experience in this world can satisfy, the most probable explanation is that I was made for another world.

C. S. Lewis, *Mere Christianity*

Chapter 2

God's Loving Quest for Us

"It pleased God, in his goodness and wisdom, to reveal himself . . ."
(*Dei Verbum*, 2).

Catechism, 51

God wants to get in touch with every human being. St. Augustine tells us what this was like in his experience:

"You called. You shouted. You broke through my deafness. You flashed, you shone and you dispelled my blindness. You breathed your fragrance on me. I drew in breath and now I pant for you. I have tasted you. Now I hunger and thirst for more. You touched me and now I burn for your peace" (*Confessions*, Book 7).

Reason pushes me to seek God. Revelation reminds me of God's drive to meet me. Reason cannot know God's inner life or his loving plan for me. I need Revelation for that. Sacred Scripture tells the story of God's progressive self-revelation for the purpose of saving me from my sins and offering me a share in divine love and life.

Scripture Records God's Self-Revelation

God began his self-revelation with our first parents. Their sin did not deter the Lord from continuous efforts to reach me. The Fourth Eucharistic Prayer says, "Again and again, you offered a covenant." A covenant is a love bond between God and us.

After making covenants with Noah, Abraham, Isaac, and Jacob, God covenanted with the people of Israel at Sinai. Through Moses, he taught them to recognize him as the only living and true God, a provident Father and a just judge.

Through the prophets, God communicated to Israel the hope of salvation: They should look for a Messiah who would establish a new and eternal covenant, intended for every person and written on the human heart. The poor and humble of heart would inherit this hope. Mary, the virgin Mother of Jesus, became their greatest personification.

The Greatest Revelation: Jesus Christ

The final Revelation and covenant took place in Jesus Christ. "In times past, God spoke in partial and various ways to our ancestors through the prophets; in these last days he spoke to us through a son, whom he made heir of all things and through whom he created the universe" (Heb 1:1-2). St. John of the Cross pointedly conveys this teaching:

"Once he has given us his Son, who is his Word, God has no other word to give us. He has said everything to us, all summed up in that unique Word. What he said partially in the prophets he has said entirely in his Son" (*Ascent of Mount Carmel*, Book II, Chapter 20).

Love demands presence. God shares divine life with me in order to be present to me as a lover to a beloved. God's self-revelation, above all in Jesus Christ, gives me an inexhaustible answer to my questions about the meaning and purpose of life, freedom from my sins, and a sharing in divine life and love.

Reflection

1. *Why did God reveal himself to us?*
   "By love, God has revealed himself and given himself to man. He has thus provided the definitive, super-abundant answer to the questions that man asks himself about the meaning and purpose of his life" (*Catechism*, 68).

2. *When did God reveal his inner life to us?*
   "Beyond the witness to himself that God gives in created things, he manifested himself to our first parents, spoke to them and, after the fall, promised them salvation (cf. Gen 3:15) and offered them his covenant.
   "God made an everlasting covenant with Noah and with all living beings (cf. Gen 9:16). It will remain in force as long as the world lasts.
   "God chose Abraham and made a covenant with him and his descendants. By the covenant God formed his people and revealed his law to them through Moses. Through the prophets, he prepared them to accept the salvation destined for all humanity" (*Catechism*, 70-72).

3. *What was God's ultimate Revelation?*
   "God has revealed himself fully by sending his own Son, in whom he has established his covenant for ever. The Son is his Father's definitive Word; so there will be no further Revelation after him" (*Catechism*, 73).

Prayer

Father, thank you for the gift of Revelation. Thank you for the Church, who teaches us what Scripture means. Thank you for Jesus Christ, the perfect expression of your self-revelation. Thank you for seeking us, loving us, saving us, and offering us a share in your life.

Resource

Catechism, 50-73

Glossary

Covenant. A love bond between God and an individual believer and between God and the Church.

Prophets. Old Testament men and women called by God to purify the faith of the people, interpret the signs of the times, and point to the future Messiah.

St. John of the Cross. A sixteenth-century mystic and writer who was involved in the reform of the Carmelite Order.

Life Application

1. Have I ever heard someone say, "That was a revelation"? What did I think when I heard the term *revelation*?
2. Since God gave me a reason which can argue for his existence, why was Revelation necessary?
3. Revelation should lead to a covenant love bond with Christ. How aware am I of my relation to Jesus? How do I work on the relationship? What should I do to deepen that covenant?

Focus

In an audience with Pope Leo XIII, Thérèse Martin begged him, "Holy Father, in honor of your jubilee, let me enter the Carmel at fifteen." A bishop intervened, "Your Holiness, the superiors are considering the request." "Very well," said the Pope, "Let the superiors decide." Thérèse clasped her hands on the Pope's knee and spoke to him as though he were her own father. "If you said yes, everyone else would be willing." Leo XIII looked at her and said, "Well . . . well . . . you will enter if it is God's will." The bishop's approval came six months later. At the age of fifteen, Thérèse entered the Carmel at Lisieux. "My dream was at last realized and peace flooded my soul."

Chapter 3

Faith Is a Dialogue of Love

> But faith is not an isolated act. No one can believe alone, just as no one can live alone.
>
> *Catechism*, 166

Faith in Jesus crucified and risen can develop from childhood to sunset years in the following ways:

(1) *The Poet.* Children are natural poets. Just as a poet sees life as a unity, so the child can believe in Jesus, his person, his message, and his Church in a unified and simple way.

(2) *The Reasoner.* As the power of reason grows, it affects our faith. Skeptical reasoning may eclipse our faith in Jesus. But positive reasoning can support our faith in Jesus.

(3) *The Personalizer.* When we are young God gives us our faith through our family, friends, and the Church. In our adult lives, Jesus asks us to believe in him in a free, true, and personal way. Personalized faith says, "I do believe, help my unbelief!" (Mk 9:24)

(4) *The Tension Bearer.* Strong faith demands testing. Jesus says: Lose the self; take the cross; follow me (cf. Mt 16:24). Holy Week reveals this plan to us. Stress, tension, and pain, when met with faith, become graced moments for closer union with Jesus.

(5) *The Easter Person.* Mature faith is like the resurrection of the child within. Once again we experience Jesus, family, society, and world as a simple unity of love rooted in God. The child has grown up and embraces all reality in the unity of faith in Jesus Christ, Son of God and son of Mary.

These faith stages are pictures of faith growth, not rigid building blocks. They come and go as we grow nearer to Jesus.

What Is Faith?

Faith is a dialogue of love with God. In Revelation, God says, "I love you." In faith, we say, "We gratefully accept your love."

This faith always has three components. First, our faith is in Jesus as a person. Second, our faith is in the message of Jesus, as given to us and interpreted by the Catholic Church. Third, faith is a motivation. We believe because Jesus has taught this or that truth. We resolve to live by this teaching because of our commitment to Christ. Hence faith is a relationship, a teaching, and a motivation.

Faith comes to us as a grace, a gift from the Holy Spirit who creates in our hearts an attraction to God. By the gift of faith, the Spirit unifies our relationship to God, our acceptance of the Gospel message, our membership in the Catholic Church, and our willingness to witness what we believe.

Faith grows powerfully by belief in the divinity of Jesus Christ. The essence of Christianity is a faith acceptance, in all its far-reaching doctrinal and practical consequences, of the divinity of Jesus Christ in the Incarnation (cf. 1 Cor 3:11).

Yes, Jesus is truly human, but it is his divinity that solicits our faith. To put faith in anything or anyone less than God is idolatry. We cannot repeat our faith, by word and deed, in Christ's divinity too often. Lord, increase our faith.

Reflection

1. *What is the "Obedience of Faith"?*

   "Faith is a personal adherence of the whole man to God who reveals himself. It involves an assent of the intellect and will to the self-revelation God has made through his deeds and words.

   " 'To believe' has thus a twofold reference: to the person and to the truth: to the truth, by trust in the person who bears witness to it" (*Catechism*, 176-177).

2. *Where does faith come from?*

   "Faith is a supernatural gift from God. In order to believe, man needs the interior helps of the Holy Spirit" (*Catechism*, 179).

3. *What is the role of reason and the Church in faith?*

   " 'Believing' is a human act, conscious and free, corresponding to the dignity of the human person.

   " 'Believing' is an ecclesial act. The Church's faith precedes, engenders, supports, and nourishes our faith" (*Catechism*, 180-181).

Prayer

Incarnate Jesus, I believe in your divinity as I behold you in the crib at Bethlehem, the carpenter's shop at Nazareth, teaching and performing miracles in Galilee, walking the way of the Cross in Jerusalem, and rising from the dead at the garden tomb. I believe in your love and salvation. Help my unbelief.

Resource

Catechism, 142-144

Glossary

Faith. A gift from God that enables us to have union with him in a personal way. Faith moves our minds to believe the revealed Word of God and is the religious motive for our behavior.

Idolatry. This gives to a created person or thing the qualities and attributes which belong to God alone.

Supernatural. Refers to the divine reality, presence, and action.

Life Application

1. Has my approach to faith changed from childhood, through adolescence into adulthood? What changes did I notice? How can I tell that my faith is deeper now than when I was younger?

2. How important are regular religious practices of devotion and prayer for my faith development? What kind of a daily prayer life do I have? What should be developed? What should be changed?

3. How often do I make faith the motive for my moral behavior? Do I act out of habit or from an ever-deeper awareness of why I do what I do? How do I examine my motives?

Focus

God showed me a little thing, the size of a hazelnut, in the palm of my hand, and it was as round as a ball. I looked at it with my mind's eye and I thought, "What can this be?" An answer came, "It is all that is made." I marveled that it could last, for I thought it might have crumbled to nothing, it was so small. And the answer came into my mind, "It lasts and ever shall because God loves it." And all things have being through the love of God.

In this little thing, I saw three truths. The first is that God made it. The second is that God loves it. The third is that God looks after it.

I can never know God until I am held so close to him that there is nothing in between.

Julian of Norwich

Chapter 4

The Holy Bible

. . . the Church has always venerated the Scriptures as she venerates the Lord's Body. She never ceases to present to the faithful the bread of life, taken from the one table of God's Word and Christ's Body.

Catechism, 103

Tolstoy's story *Where Love Is, There Is God Also* vividly illustrates the gift of Scripture. In this story, Martin, the main character, is devastated by the death of his wife. Only reading the Gospel consoled him. Each time he read a chapter, warmth flooded his heart and despair subsided.

One day he read the story of Simon the Pharisee refusing hospitality to Jesus. Martin thought, "If Jesus ever came to my home, I would welcome him with all my heart." At that very moment he heard the words, "Martin, I am coming to your home tomorrow."

Convinced that Jesus was coming, Martin prepared his house for Jesus. The next day he was visited by a tired soldier, a poor woman with her baby, and an old woman with a young boy. Martin treated each of these with affection and hospitality. But he was disappointed. Jesus never came.

That evening, he opened his Bible and read from Matthew 25, "I was hungry and you fed me. I was naked and you clothed me. I was sick and you consoled me." Martin noticed a special light had filled his room. Joyously, Martin realized Jesus had indeed come to him in the presence of the needy visitors he had helped that day.

Just as Martin in this story found Jesus in Scripture as well as in his acts of love, so also do we. In the previous chapters we have outlined the basis for our relationship with God. We are born with a capacity for God and an inner drive toward him. This is not a useless passion because God comes toward us with even greater joy and love. This coming of God to us is found in Revelation.

How is this Revelation communicated to us? Through the Bible and Tradition. " '*Sacred Scripture* is the speech of God as it is put down in writing under the breath of the Holy Spirit' (*Dei Verbum*, 9). 'And [Holy] *Tradition* transmits in its entirety the Word of God which has been entrusted to the apostles by Christ the Lord and the Holy Spirit. It transmits to the successors of the apostles so that, enlightened by the Spirit of truth, they may faithfully preserve, expound, and spread it abroad by their preaching' (*Dei Verbum*, 9)" (*Catechism*, 81-82).

Scripture and Tradition flow from the one source, a revealing God. The Church does not derive her certainty about Revelation's truths from the Bible alone. Both Scripture and Tradition must be accepted with equal attention and reverence. The *Catechism*, in paragraphs 84-95, outlines the way our faith heritage should be interpreted.

Among all the books of Scripture, the Gospels hold a special place of honor for us, because they tell us about Jesus Christ, his person and his message. The Gospels we read now were formed in three stages:

(1) *The life and teachings of Jesus.* The Church clearly affirms the historicity of the four Gospels. They faithfully hand on what Jesus, the Son of God, really did and taught for our salvation, during his life among us until his ascension (cf. *Catechism*, 126).

(2) *The oral Tradition.* What Jesus Christ said and did, the apostles preached to others. They brought to their preaching a deeper knowledge of what they experienced, instructed by the glorious events of Christ and enlightened by the Spirit of truth.

(3) *The written Gospels.* "The Sacred authors composed the four Gospels, choosing certain of the numerous elements handed down, either orally or already in writing, editing a synthesis of others, or explaining them in terms of the Church's current situation, and finally keeping the form of preaching, in such a way as always to deliver the honest truth about Jesus to us" (*Catechism*, 126 and *Dei Verbum*, 19; Second Vatican Council, hereafter referred to as SVC).

The strength and power of God's Word provides support and energy for all the Church's members. It gives us a stronger faith, food for our souls, and a rich source for our spiritual life. The study of Scripture should be the soul of theological studies. Teaching religion, preaching homilies, or evangelizing others derives its power, dynamism, and effectiveness from constant contact with Scripture. Studying Scripture is essential for knowing and loving Jesus Christ.

Reflection
What are the three criteria for interpreting Scripture in accord with the Spirit who inspired it?

"1. *Be especially attentive 'to the content and unity of the whole Scripture.'* Different as the books which comprise it may be, Scripture is a unity by reason of the unity of God's plan, of which Christ Jesus is the center and heart, open since his Passover. . . .

"2. *Read the Scripture within 'the living Tradition of the whole Church.'* According to a saying of the Fathers, Sacred Scripture is written principally in the Church's heart rather than in documents and records, for the Church carries in her Tradition the living memorial of God's Word, and it is the Holy Spirit who gives her the spiritual interpretation of the Scripture. . . .

"3. *Be attentive to the analogy of faith.* By 'analogy of faith' we mean the coherence of the truths of faith among themselves and within the whole plan of Revelation" (*Catechism*, 112-114).

Prayer

Father, we love you for coming to us and responding to the desire for you which you have planted in our minds and hearts. We thank you for communicating your Revelation in Scripture and Tradition. We treasure the Scriptures, especially the Gospels, which tell us so much about Jesus Christ, Son of God and Savior. But more than this, we praise you for speaking to us with love through the pages of Scripture as taught to us by our Spirit-guided Church.

Resource

Catechism, 74-141

Glossary

Analogy of Faith. "The coherence of the truths of faith among themselves and within the whole plan of Revelation" (*Catechism*, 114).

Canon of Scripture. Guided by the apostolic Tradition, the Church discerned which writings were to be included in the Bible. The list is called the "canon of Scripture."

Life Application

1. How often do I read the Bible? How frequently do I think I should read it? Which parts of the Bible appeal to me the most? Why? What do I look for in Scripture? How does my reading of Scripture help me to pray?

2. It is said that people who read Scripture have a greater desire to share their faith with others. How true is this in my life? Who are some relatives and friends I would like to bring back to the Church? What do I find in Scripture devotion which helps me be motivated to share my faith?

3. Why is it important to know the three principles of scriptural interpretation given above in the reflection? How clearly do I appreciate the need to have the Church's guidance in reading Scripture?

Focus

The Church, as early as apostolic times, and then constantly in her Tradition, has illuminated the unity of the divine plan in the two Testaments through typology, which discerns in God's works of the Old Covenant prefigurations of what he accomplished in the fullness of time in the person of his incarnate Son.

Christians therefore read the Old Testament in the light of Christ crucified and risen. Such typological reading discloses the inexhaustible content of the Old Testament; but it must not make us forget that [it] retains its own intrinsic value as Revelation reaffirmed by our Lord himself. Besides, the New Testament has to be read in the light of the Old. Early Christian catechesis made constant use of the Old Testament. As an old saying put it, the New Testament lies hidden in the Old and the Old Testament is unveiled in the New.

Catechism, 128-129

Chapter 5

I Believe in God

"I believe in God": this first affirmation of the Apostles' Creed is also the most fundamental.

Catechism, 199

"Nine in ten Americans say they have never doubted the existence of God and eight in ten believe they will face God on Judgment Day. Eight in ten also believe that God works miracles today and say they are 'sometimes very conscious of God.' 90 percent of Americans pray and 88 percent believe that God loves them" (*The People's Religion*, pp. 45, 56).

The *Catechism of the Catholic Church* begins with an explanation of the creed, the faith professed by Catholics. And the first statement of the creed is about faith in God. A creed summarizes what Catholics believe. The two creeds most often used are the Apostles' Creed and the Nicene Creed.

The Apostles' Creed is considered to be a summary of the faith of the apostles. It is the ancient baptismal creed of the Church of Rome. The Nicene Creed was composed at the first two ecumenical councils — Nicaea in 325 and Constantinople in 381. We pray this creed at our celebration of the Eucharist.

Faith in God

Faith affirms there is only one God. God asks the world to come to him alone. "Turn to me and be safe" (Isa 45:22). Jesus teaches that God is the only Lord and we should love him (see Mk 12:29-30).

Because our faith experiences the boundless love of God for us, it moves us to return that love. Our faith motivates us to love all people because God loves them. We use creation to draw nearer to God and we avoid what separates us from the Lord.

Who Is God?

Moses met God at the burning bush. God commissioned him to save his people from slavery. Moses told God that his people would wonder about the name of the one who sent him. God replied, "[T]ell the Israelites, I AM sent me to you" (read Ex 3:4-14).

In Scripture, the name expresses the essence of the person. God is not an abstract force or a vague destiny. God is an "I" to whom we can and must reply. This powerful "I" of God promises to hear our cries for love and mercy and save us. The "I Am" means God is always here, faithfully present to care for us.

At the same time, God remains a holy mystery. At the burning bush, Moses took off his sandals and bowed in reverence. God reveals and conceals himself. We can never know fully the immense mystery of God. God alone IS. We become. We grow from childhood to old age. God IS. What we are we have from God. The bush burned without being consumed. God IS.

Ultimately the answer to God's identity is love. God is love.

"Whoever is without love does not know God, for God is love" (1 Jn 4:8). Jesus reveals and fully realizes the name of God given to Moses at the burning bush. On the Cross that divine love-name burst forth like the sun. "When you lift up the Son of Man [on the Cross], then you will realize that I AM" (Jn 8:28).

In all the Easter narratives, the risen Jesus requires faith in order to know him. Our spiritual journey always begins with faith: "I believe in God."

Reflection

1. *Why does our faith speak of "one" God?*
   " 'Hear, O Israel, the LORD our God is one LORD . . .' (Deut 6:4; Mk 12:29)" (*Catechism*, 228).

2. *What does our faith in God mean for us?*
   "Faith in God leads us to turn to him alone as our first origin and our ultimate goal, and neither to prefer anything to him nor to substitute anything for him" (*Catechism*, 229).

3. *Can we know God completely?*
   "Even when he reveals himself, God remains a mystery beyond words: 'If you understood him, it would not be God' (St. Augustine, *Sermo* 52, 6, 16: PL 38:360 and *Sermo* 117, 3, 5: PL 38, 663)" (*Catechism*, 230).

Prayer

I believe in you, my God. I praise you for revealing yourself to us as I AM, an "I" who loves and cares for us. I praise your majesty and exult in your glory. I ask you to help me never to refuse you anything. I need your help to make you the beginning and end of all I am and have. Glory be to you, O God.

Resource

Catechism, 185-231

Glossary

Apostles' Creed. A true summary of the faith of the apostles. It is the ancient baptismal creed of the Church.

I AM. The name of God revealed to Moses at the burning bush.

Mystery. When applied to God, this term implies some insight into God's inner life. At the same time, we will never know God fully in this world.

Nicene Creed. This was composed at the first two ecumenical councils, Nicaea in 325 and First Constantinople in 381. We use it at our Sunday Eucharists.

Life Application

1. Suppose I met someone who said that faith in God is unimportant. What would I say? Would I try to argue the person into faith? If so, what arguments would I use? Or would I ask the person to explain his resistance to believing in God?

2. How can I tell from my own experience that God is mystery? Generally, what do I know about God? What don't I know? How could prayer help me know God better?

3. What should I do to deepen my faith in God? How does the Church help me with my faith? How do my family and friends advance my faith in God?

Focus

I seek not, O Lord, to search out Thy depth, but I desire in some measure to understand Thy truth, which my heart believeth and loveth. Nor do I seek to understand that I may believe, but I believe that I may understand. For this too I believe, that unless I first believe, I shall not understand.

. . . right order requires that we believe the deep things of the Christian religion before presuming to subject them to the . . . test of reason, so on the other hand it looks to me like indolent neglect if, already established in the faith, we do not take the trouble to gain an intellectual intimacy with what we believe.

St. Anselm in *English Spirituality*

Chapter 6

Trinity — God as a Community

> "Above all guard for me this great deposit of faith for which I live and fight. . . . I mean the profession of faith in the Father and the Son and the Holy Spirit" (St. Gregory Nazianzen).

Catechism, 256

Millions love mystery stories. They read Agatha Christie and watch "Murder, She Wrote." Solving the mystery causes the pleasure. Some mysteries intrigue us because they have not been solved. Why did the dinosaurs die out? Was it lack of room in Noah's ark? Did a cosmic star hit the earth like a neutron bomb and kill all the dinosaurs? We do not know. This is an unsolved mystery.

Our faith encounters another mystery, God as a Holy Trinity. Why do we believe God is Trinity? Because God told us. Jesus teaches us God is Father. "Father, the hour has come" (Jn 17:1). At the Last Supper Jesus spoke of God as Father forty-five times.

In turn, the Father tells us he has a Son. When Jesus was baptized in the Jordan, the Father spoke from heaven and said, "You are my beloved Son; with you I am well pleased" (Lk 3:22).

Lastly, God is Holy Spirit. Jesus said, "I will ask the Father, and he will give you another Advocate . . . the Spirit of truth" (Jn 14:16). The Spirit is more than an abstract energy. The Spirit is a divine person.

God is Father, Son, Spirit. Three persons. One God. God is one divine nature in three divine persons. God is not just one person. Nor is God three natures.

We owe the use of person and nature to speak of the Trinity to two ecumenical councils, Nicaea in 325 and First Constantinople in 381. A Libyan-born priest named Arius was preaching that Jesus was not divine. He taught that God created a Logos, a Word, through which he made the world. When the world needed redemption, the created Word took flesh in Jesus. To reward him for his fine work, God "adopted" Jesus and made him a minor divinity to be honored more than other people.

Three hundred and eighteen bishops attended the Council of Nicaea to counter Arius. They taught that Jesus, the Word made flesh, was of the same divine substance as the Father and not a created minor divinity. They published a creed that said so.

That creed also said, "I believe in the Holy Spirit." It did not say the Spirit was God. The Arians began to teach that the Holy Spirit was not God.

So the bishops held another council at Constantinople and explicitly taught the Spirit was God: "We believe in the Holy Spirit, the Lord, the giver of life."

Scripture already had this teaching. The faith of the Church always held it. Councils were needed to *reaffirm* it. In our own day, the *Catechism of the Catholic Church* is needed to spell this out again. God is a Trinity of three divine persons in one divine nature. God is love. The Father loves the Son. The Son loves the Father. The Spirit is the love between them, so real that the Spirit is a divine person.

Community occurs in the Trinity and models communal love for us. If God is a community, then we should be as well.

Reflection

1. *How important is the teaching about the Trinity?*

   "The mystery of the Most Holy Trinity is the central mystery of the Christian faith and of Christian life. God alone can make it known to us by revealing himself as Father, Son, and Holy Spirit" (*Catechism*, 261).

2. *Which sacrament first brings us to the Trinity?*

   "By the grace of Baptism 'in the name of the Father and of the Son and of the Holy Spirit,' we are called to share in the life of the Blessed Trinity, here on earth in the obscurity of faith, and after death in eternal light (cf. Paul VI, *Solemn Profession of Faith*)" (*Catechism*, 265).

3. *Which councils give us the teaching about the Trinity?*

   ". . . the Church confessed at the first ecumenical council at Nicaea (325) that the Son is "consubstantial" with the Father, that is, one only God with him."

   "Before his Passover, Jesus announced the sending of 'another Paraclete' (Advocate), the Holy Spirit. . . . The Holy Spirit is thus revealed as another divine person with Jesus and the Father" (*Catechism*, 242, 243).

Prayer

Glory to the Father, and to the Son, and to the Holy Spirit: as it was in the beginning, is now, and will be forever. Amen.

Resource

Catechism, 232-265

Glossary

First Constantinople. Name of the Church's second council in 381, at which the divinity of the Holy Spirit was reaffirmed.

Holy Trinity. God is a Trinity of three divine persons in one divine nature.

Nature. The center of operation, the "what" does it.

Nicaea. City where the first council of the Church was held in 325. The bishops reaffirmed the Church's traditional faith in the divinity of Christ against Arius who denied it.

Person. The center of responsibility, the "who" does it.

Life Application

1. God the Father is my creator. What then should my attitude be as a creature in reference to my heavenly Father? How often do I thank God for the gift of life?
2. The Son of God is my redeemer. How do I experience the need for salvation? When I pray to Jesus about my salvation, what themes do I bring up?
3. The Holy Spirit is my sanctifier. How committed am I to a holy life? What virtues help me to be holy? How is the Holy Spirit helping me to be dedicated to the journey to holiness?

Focus

. . . the very structure of human language is bound up with the distinction [of person and nature]; if you ask, "Who is that?" the answer is "John"; if you ask, "What is that?" the answer is, "a man." The word "who" refers to the person, the word "what" to the nature.

The doctrine of the Trinity thus means that there is one single mind and one single will in God, which is three times focussed: think of an infinite circle with a triple super-imposed center. If you said to God, "What are you?" he would reply, "God." If you said, "Who are you?" there would be a threefold "I — I am the Father, I am the Son, I am the Spirit."

Frank Sheed and Maisie Ward,
Catholic Evidence Training Outlines

Chapter 7

Why Do We Call God Our 'Father'?

Jesus revealed that God is Father in an unheard-of sense: he is Father not only in being Creator; he is eternally Father in relation to his only Son, who is eternally Son only in relation to his Father.

Catechism, 240

We live in a time of the absent father. Countless divorces have exiled fathers from the lives of their children. Even where marriages are intact, many fathers functionally abandon their children by absorption in their work. It has been said that such fathers spend no more than ten minutes a day being present to their children. In the doctrine of God as Father, we have the opportunity to rebuild God's call to human fatherhood.

Jesus tells us that God is Father. It has already been noted that Jesus spoke of God as Father forty-five times in the Last Supper Discourse. Jesus tells us that God's name is Father. "I have made your name known" (Jn 17:6; JB). The people of Israel had already praised God as Father and thanked him for adopting them as his favorite children (see Ex 4:22).

No human has ever seen God directly. Only the Son of God has done so, because he lived in the "bosom of the Father." That is why he could reveal him (Jn 1:18). At Gethsemane, when Jesus agonized over the suffering that our salvation would require, he talked to God as Father, even using the affectionate and intimate term "*Abba*," or Papa. In the last of his seven words from the Cross, Christ's final address to God was as Father.

Who is God the Father of? God is Father of his only Son. Deep inside the mystery of divinity, Father and Son have a reciprocal relationship. They know and love each other with absolute intimacy. How do we know this? Because Jesus told us, and we believe he is telling us the truth (Mt 11:27).

In this era of inclusive language, should we not call God a parent? Are not the scriptural terms applied to God just poetic comparisons borrowed from the culture of the times? In some cases, yes. But not here. Jesus, the Son of God, says God is Father. Either we believe him or we don't. The idea of God as Father is not derived from earthly fatherhood. Just the opposite. The idea of an earthly father is adapted from our heavenly Father.

This in no way diminishes woman or motherhood. The most revered human being in history is Mary, a woman and a mother. The greatest choice ever made by a mere human was the decision made by a woman/mother to accept the divine call to conceive the Savior of the world by the Spirit's power.

Secular wisdom tries to make it plausible to deny God as Father. But our religion does not arise from the secular culture. Our faith comes from God, who compassionately came to us and told us about his inner life.

What does God's Fatherhood mean? Three things: (1) God is the divine Father of the divine Son; (2) Our Father makes us in his image; (3) Our Father shares his divine life and love with us. We become images of God simply by being born. We become adopted sons and daughters of God by being born again in faith and Baptism.

The doctrine of God as Father calls us to restore the active role of human fatherhood. God the Father is creative, vital, and generative. Human families need these essential values. Our heavenly Father calls for earthly, caring fathers. Children deserve them. The hope of families and culture depends on them.

Reflection

1. *What are the three meanings of God as Father?*

   "In Israel, God is called 'Father' inasmuch as he is Creator of the world. Even more, God is Father because of the covenant and the gift of the law to Israel, 'his first-born son' (Ex 4:22)."

   "Jesus revealed that God is Father . . . by his relationship to his only Son who is eternally Son only in relation to his Father" (*Catechism*, 238, 240).

2. *Did Jesus speak of God only as Creator?*

   "Jesus revealed that God is Father . . . by his relationship to his only Son who is eternally Son only in relation to his Father" (*Catechism*, 240).

3. *In what various ways do the apostles speak of Jesus as the Father's Son?*

   ". . . the apostles confess Jesus to be the Word: 'In the beginning was the Word, and the Word was with God, and the Word was God' (Jn 1:1); as 'the image of the invisible God' (Col 1:15)" (*Catechism*, 241).

Prayer

God, we rejoice to call you Father because Jesus has made this possible. As Father, you created us and in Jesus made us your adopted sons and daughters through faith and Baptism. Our humanity flourishes because of you and our share in your divine life increases our joy. *Abba*, we love you.

Resource

Catechism, 238-242, 441-445

Glossary

God as Father. God is the divine Father of the divine Son. God as Father-Creator makes us in his image. God's saving work in Jesus and the Spirit adopts us as sons and daughters through grace and sacraments.

Life Application

1. The absence of fatherhood due to death, divorce, or neglect deprives children of an important nurturing influence. What can be done to supplement the missing father? How does our faith in God our Father inspire us in this regard?
2. What can we learn about fatherhood from Christ's intimate ways of speaking of his filial relation to his "*Abba* (Papa), Father"?
3. How do mothering and fathering complement each other? What was my own experience of my parents in this matter? How do I handle my parenting responsibilities?

Focus

What sort of person is God? . . . He is "the Father." When we hear this familiar truth we nearly always read back into God's character what we know of fatherhood. This is understandable enough, but it reverses the actual truth. If God is "the Father," . . . then we derive (if we are parents) our characteristics from Him. We are reproducing, no doubt on a microscopic scale and in a thoroughly faulty manner, something of the Character of God. If once we accept it as true that the whole Power behind this astonishing Universe is of that kind of character that Christ could only describe as "Father," the whole of life is transfigured. . . . People, and our relationships with them, at once become of tremendous importance. . . . [It] is people not things that matter.

J. B. Phillips, *Your God Is Too Small*

Chapter 8

The Creation – 'Like Looking at God'

Creation is the foundation of "all God's saving plans," the "beginning of the history of salvation" that culminates in Christ.

Catechism, 280

In the spring of 1992, astrophysicist George Smoot detected slight fluctuations in the universe's cosmic radiation. He believes these are echoes of the Big Bang, the moment of creation. "If you're religious," he told reporters, "this is like looking at God."

Modern science may be waking up to what faith has held all along. "In the beginning God created the heavens and the earth" (Gn 1:1; JB). The very first sentence in the Bible tells us that God created the universe. Our faith affirms that God created the world and all that is in it. "It is by faith we understand that the world was created by one word from God" (Heb 11:3; JB).

Other religions and philosophies have different views of how creation happened. Some ancient Chinese believed the world was born from the dark womb of Yin, a female goddess. Others say that a god made the world out of available materials, such as Marduk making it from the corpse of Tiamat. Some Greek philosophers argued the world was an emanation from God. Some modern New Age pantheists say the world is an expression of the divine mind.

Catholic teaching is quite different. God made the world out of *nothing.* He did not make the world out of *anything.* We create things out of existing materials. We make a suit from wool, a house from wood, and a statue from marble. We use a process to make things. God simply spoke and things appeared. "Then God said, 'Let there be light,' and there was light" (Gn 1:3).

God created freely. Nothing forced him to make the world. The universe is not an emanation from God, like light from a star. God acted out of sheer goodness. God continues to maintain and support the world. We call this loving act "divine providence." Deism says that God made the world like a clock and let it run on its own. Our faith in his providence denies this. "In him, we live and move and have our being" (Acts 17:28).

God made us for his glory. This does not mean God is like an actor wanting cheers from his audience. God's glory happens when people achieve the goal for which they were made. The goal is love and salvation. When this appears in us, God's glory — his presence and love — shines in the world.

Divine providence not only sustains the world but produces a plan for divine salvation to occur in history through the saving work of Jesus Christ. We discover divine providence by surrendering with faith and confidence to the watchful care and plan of God. This does not mean passivity or fatalism. God calls us to live freely, consciously, and responsibly. God's loving grace and our constant prayer make this attitude possible.

Our response to creation should be a song of praise. "Come, let us sing joyfully to the Lord. . . . / His is the sea, for he has made it, / and the dry land, which his hands have formed" (Ps 95:1, 5).

Reflection

1. *What is the first lesson creation teaches us?*
    "In the creation of the world and of man, God gave the first and universal witness to his almighty love and his wisdom, the first proclamation of the 'plan of his loving goodness,' which finds its goal in the new creation in Christ" (*Catechism*, 315).

2. *What does it mean to say God "creates"?*
    "God alone created the universe freely, directly, and without any help.
    "No creature has the infinite power necessary to 'create' . . . to produce and give being to that which had in no way possessed it" (*Catechism*, 317-318).

3. *What is the link between creation and God's glory?*
    "God created the world to show forth and communicate his glory. That his creatures should share in his truth, goodness, and beauty — this is the glory for which God created them" (*Catechism*, 319).

Prayer

All creatures of our God and King.
Lift up your voices let us sing. Alleluia!
Bright burning sun with golden beams
Soft silver moon that gently gleams.
O praise him. Alleluia.
From St. Francis of Assisi

Resource

Catechism, 279-321

Glossary

Creation. God alone created the universe and all it contains, out of nothing, freely, directly, and with no help.

Deism. A philosophy that says God created the world with all it needs to develop itself with no providential care needed from him nor any salvation by Christ. God is like a clockmaker: he wound the world up and let it run completely on its own.

Divine Providence. By his providence, God sustains the world he created and initiated the plan of salvation which was accomplished by Jesus Christ.

Pantheism. A philosophy that claims we are all part of God, and not distinct from him.

Life Application

1. Why is the teaching that God created the world important for my life? What difference does it make? Suppose I did not believe it, what effect would that have on my life?
2. Why is the teaching about divine providence valuable for my daily life? What would I say to someone who agreed that God created the world, but has no further involvement in what goes on here?
3. If I met a New Age pantheist, what might I bring up which could persuade him or her to see our belief in creation and the difference between God and created beings?

Focus

The universe is thought to be about fifteen billion years old. The earth was formed some four and a half billion years ago, and life has been on earth close to four billion years. Conjectures about the origin of human life have changed enormously in the past three decades. . . .

It is difficult to conceive of such long periods of time. If we let a single sheet of paper represent a million years, a volume of one thousand sheets (that is, two thousand pages) would represent a billion years. This is approximately the size of the Oxford Annotated Bible. Four and a half such bibles would represent just the age of the earth. The entire fossil record of mankind would come on the last three sheets. If the pages are divided into two columns, with about fifty lines of print to a column (like the OAB), the last line of the last column of the last page would represent five thousand years, enough to include all of recorded history (that is, from 3000 B.C. to A.D. 2000), and that last line would not yet be completely filled out.

Edward O'Connor, C.S.C., *The Catholic Vision*

Chapter 9

Man and Woman
– A Little Less Than the Angels

"Being man" or "being woman" is a reality which is good and willed by God.

Catechism, 369

Many cultures have believed in the existence of a soul distinct from the body. Ancient Egyptians called it "Ka." The Coola Indians of British Columbia imagine it to be like a bird. Native peoples of Brazil and Guyana consider dreams to be adventures of the soul that leaves the body during sleep. Jesus referred to the soul when he said, "And do not be afraid of those who kill the body but cannot kill the soul" (Mt 10:28).

Catholics believe in the reality of the spiritual soul, connected to, but different from, the body. This flows from the creation teaching about man and woman being "images of God." Psychobiology demonstrates the link between the human psyche and animals. We resemble beasts in their aggressiveness, courtship rituals, and territorial imperatives. But we are more than beasts.

Scripture emphasizes our link with God. We are made a "little less than the angels" (Ps 8:6). We have some kinship with animals, but God made us human and able to relate to him. We are the only creatures able to share, by knowledge and love, in God's own life. This happens because we have spiritual souls.

The human soul as an image of God possesses four qualities: intelligence, love, freedom, and conscience. God creates each of our souls when we are conceived. Our souls are immortal and do not perish at death when separated temporarily from our bodies.

The body also shares in the dignity of being an image of God because it "is intended to become, in the body of Christ, a temple of the Spirit" (*Catechism*, 364). God will raise our bodies from the dead on the Last Day.

Further, God created man and woman. God is the author of masculinity and femininity, of sexual and gender differences. As husband and wife, man and woman should relate to one another as a communion of persons who reflect the communion of love in the persons of the Trinity. Their love overcomes loneliness.

Such a love rests on absolute fidelity in imitation of God. This love should be creative and generative, producing new human life as the Creator has willed and raising children to live out their divine and human calling. God also called man and woman to be stewards of creation, loving all that exists and nourishing its potential. Mastery of self prepares for mastery of creation.

The Son of God showed us how precious humanity is by being born the son of Mary. Jesus Christ reveals to us the fullness of human dignity. "Christ the Lord, Christ the new Adam . . . fully reveals man to himself and brings to light his most high calling" (*Gaudium et Spes*, 22; SVC).

The best path to human fulfillment is obedience to Christ's teachings and becoming his disciple by losing self, taking the cross, and following him. Then the dream of creation becomes real in us. Our life with Jesus becomes Paradise regained.

Reflection

1. *Why are we called "images of God"?*

   " 'God created man in his image . . . male and female he created them' (Gn 1:27)."

   "Of all visible creatures only man is 'able to know and love his creator' (*Gaudium et Spes*, 12). He is 'the only creature on earth that God has willed for its own sake' (*Gaudium et Spes*, 24), and he alone is called to share by knowledge and love, in God's own life."

   "In Sacred Scripture the term 'soul' . . . refers to the innermost aspect of man, that which is of greatest value in him, that by which he is most especially in God's image. . . ."

   "The human body shares in the dignity of 'the image of God': . . . and it is the whole human person that is intended to become, in the body of Christ, a temple of the Spirit" (*Catechism*, 355, 356, 363, 364).

2. *Why did God create male and female?*

   "Man and woman were made 'for each other' — not that God left them half-made and incomplete: he created them to be a communion of persons, in which each can be 'helpmate' to the other, for they are equal as persons . . . and complementary as masculine and feminine. In marriage God unites them in such a way that, by forming 'one flesh,' they can transmit human life: 'Be fruitful and multiply, and fill the earth.' By transmitting human life to their descendants, man and woman as spouses and parents cooperate in a unique way in the Creator's work" (*Catechism*, 372).

3. *What do we know of the original state of humans?*

   "Revelation makes known to us the state of original holiness and justice of man and woman before sin: from their friendship with God flowed the happiness of their existence in paradise" (*Catechism*, 384).

Prayer

Loving God, you honored us by creating us in your image so we could know and love you and share your life. We praise you for this great human dignity and most precious gift.

Resource

Catechism, 355-384

Glossary

Discipleship. Applied to those who follow the command of Christ to lose the self, take the cross, and follow him.

Images of God. We image God in our souls, which possess intelligence, love, freedom, and conscience. We also image God in our bodies which, in the Body of Christ, are called to be temples of the Holy Spirit.

Original Justice. The state of man and woman before the Fall.

Life Application

1. If I image God in my soul's capacity to know, love, act freely, and make moral judgments based on an informed conscience, how am I doing right now? How should I exercise these four soul qualities more effectively?
2. Despite cultural efforts toward unisex and gender bending (that is, dissolving differences between genders), why did God create masculinity and femininity? How can I best be me and still respect the opposite sex?
3. How does my vision of myself as an image of God help me to respect the human dignity and freedom of others?

Focus

(The following is from an interview with Mother Teresa, "A Pencil In the Hand of God," *Time*, December 4, 1989.)

What did you do this morning?
Pray.

When did you start?
Half past four.

And after prayer?
We try to pray through our work by doing it with Jesus, for Jesus, to Jesus. That helps us put our whole heart and soul into doing it.

The dying, the crippled, the mentally ill, the unwanted, the unloved —
they are Jesus in disguise. . . .

You feel you have no special qualities?
I don't think so. . . . It is [God's] work. I am like a little pencil in his hand. . . .
He does the thinking. He does the writing. . . .

How do you find rich people. . . ?
I find the rich much poorer. . . . They are never satisfied. . . . I don't say all
of them are like that. . . . I find that poverty hard to remove. The hunger for
love is much more difficult to remove than the hunger for bread.

Chapter 10

Original Sin

Scripture portrays the tragic consequences of this first disobedience. Adam and Eve immediately lose the grace of original holiness.

Catechism, 399

Some years ago the London *Times* asked some authors to write essays on the topic, "What's Wrong With The World?" Catholic convert Gilbert Chesterton, wrote the briefest reply:

> Dear Sirs:
> I am.
> Sincerely Yours,
> G. K. Chesterton

No one is perfect. An honest look at our own experience reveals we are sinners all. Why is this so? Were we always sinners? Genesis 1-3 gives us God's answer. Scripture tells the history of the Fall of Man in the language of imagery. God created Adam and Eve in his own image, endowed with intelligence, love, freedom, and conscience. He gave them the grace of original holiness that made it possible for them to be friends with him. They began in grace, not sin.

God tested that friendship by forbidding them to eat of the tree of the knowledge of good and evil. "The moment you eat of it, you are surely doomed to die" (Gn 2:17). What did the test mean? The tree symbolized the limits of humans as creatures. We should depend on and be subject to God's moral laws which govern our freedom. God was testing the use of human freedom.

Adam and Eve used their freedom to disobey God's command. Disobedience was the first sin and is characteristic of all sins thereafter. Scripture vividly describes the outcome of the first sin: (1) the loss of the grace of sharing in God's life; (2) the loss of inner harmony between body, passions, will, and mind; (3) division, strife, domination, greed, suffering; (4) death.

St. Paul says that "through one person sin entered the world, and through sin, death" (Rom 5:12). It was St. Augustine who coined the term "original sin" to refer to the impact of the sin of our first parents on us. It caused the death of the body. It also caused the wounds of human nature.

St. Thomas speaks of these four wounds as: (1) ignorance, meaning difficulty in knowing truth and loss of confidence that it can be known; (2) malice in the mind, inclining us to uncharitable motives; (3) weakness in the will, making it difficult to choose goodness; (4) disorder in our passions and emotions, causing us to lose control of ourselves.

We do not commit original sin. We only commit actual sins. But we are born with the effects of original sin, alienated from God and wounded in body and soul. That is why the Church requires Baptism even for infants who have committed no actual sins. Baptism gives us the grace of Christ and restores our friendship with God. The wounds of original sin remain, but through grace and spiritual struggle, we have a lifetime to overcome the effects of this sin.

God did not abandon our first parents or the human race. From the very beginning, God promised a savior (Gn 3:9-15). The Son of God fulfilled that promise in his Incarnation and redemption.

Reflection

1. *What was the first sin?*
   " 'Although set by God in a state of rectitude, man, enticed by the evil one, abused his freedom at the very start of history. He lifted himself up against God and sought to attain his goal apart from him' " (*Gaudium et Spes*, 13; *Catechism*, 415).

2. *What was the effect of this first sin?*
   "By his sin Adam, as the first man, lost the original holiness and justice he received from God, not only for himself but for all human beings" (*Catechism*, 416).

3. *What is original sin?*
   "Adam and Eve transmitted to their descendants human nature wounded by their own first sin and hence deprived of original holiness and justice; this deprivation is called 'original sin' " (*Catechism*, 417).

Prayer

Father, how wonderful your care for us!
How boundless your merciful love!
To ransom a slave
you gave away your Son.

O happy fault, O necessary sin of Adam,
which gained for us so great a Redeemer!

. . . Rejoice, O Mother Church!
The risen Savior shines upon you!
                    Easter Vigil, Exsultet, *Sacramentary*

Resource

Catechism, 385-417

Glossary

Original Holiness. The state of graced friendship with God given to Adam and Eve prior to the Fall.

Original Sin. Adam and Eve's act of disobedience to God's command not to eat the forbidden fruit. We experience its effects as a deprivation of original holiness. We are restored to God's friendship by the graces of faith and Baptism.

Wounds of Original Sin. Four wounds of ignorance, malice, weakness of the will, disordered passions.

Life Application

1. Faith and Baptism have delivered me from original sin, but its wounds remain — difficulty in knowing and learning truth, for example. When I look back on my years of education, how did this fact affect me?
2. At the end of each day, what do I notice about the difference between what I intended and what I actually did? How can I improve my choice of the good with God's help? How can I keep my resolutions?
3. Like others, my emotions and passions cloud my mind and overwhelm my willpower. What examples of this come to me? What will I do about it? How can I balance the positive values of my feelings with thinking and acting?

Focus

The secret of my ministry is in that crucifix you see opposite my bed. It's there so that I can see it in my first waking moment and before going to sleep. It's there, also, so that I can talk to it during the long evening hours. Look at it. See it as I see it. Those open arms have been the programme of my pontificate: they say that Christ died for all, for all. No one is excluded from his love, from his forgiveness.

In this last hour I feel calm and sure that my Lord in his mercy will not reject me. I've done my best to pay homage to truth, justice, charity, and the meek and humble heart of the Gospel. My time on earth is drawing to a close. But Christ lives on and the Church continues his work. Souls . . . Souls . . . Save them.

Pope John XXIII

Chapter 11

Praise the Son of God

> "The Church . . . believes that the key, the center, and the purpose of the whole of man's history is to be found in its Lord and Master" (*Gaudium et Spes*, 10).
>
> *Catechism*, 450

An Irish woman from Galway kept dreaming of a treasure under a bridge in Dublin. So one day she traveled there to find the money. It wasn't there. Disappointed, she discussed this with a policeman. He laughed and said, "Pay no attention to dreams. Why, last night I dreamt about a money box in a bedroom in Galway."

Unwittingly, he was describing this lady's room. He said, "Of course, no one believes in dreams." She raced back home and found the treasure. She had traveled far to find what was right under her nose.

Jesus Christ is the treasure hidden in the room of our Church and our spirit. We look for Christ-substitutes everywhere except in him who is our center and hope. Who is Jesus? He is the Son of God. He is the son of Mary. He is our Savior. We will look at his divinity in this lesson and his humanity and saving work in the next lessons.

The New Testament teaches that Jesus is the Son of God. At Caesarea Philippi, Peter says of Jesus, "You are the Messiah, the Son of the living God" (Mt 16:16). Jesus replies that Peter knows this, not from human reasoning, but because the Father has revealed this truth to him.

On two solemn occasions in the Gospels, the Baptism of Jesus and the Transfiguration, the voice of the Father is heard.

The Father speaks of Jesus as his "beloved Son" (Mt 3:17; 17:5). Jesus speaks of himself as the only Son of God (Jn 3:16). He tells of his preexistence as Son of God in John 10:36.

At the same time, Jesus often addressed God as Father. In the Gospels, the term *father* is applied to God 170 times. Jesus speaks of his Father as "*Abba*" (Mk 14:36). This Aramaic form of father is equivalent to the English "daddy" or "papa." Not only children used it, but older people also out of respect for a venerable person. Jesus practiced and taught a uniquely intimate relationship with God.

"Yes, Father, such as been your gracious will. All things have been handed over to me by my Father. No one knows the Son except the Father, and no one knows the Father except the Son and those to whom the Son wishes to reveal him" (Mt 11:26-27).

His listeners understood what he was saying. Why else did they accuse him of blasphemy? "For this reason the Jews tried all the more to kill him, because he not only broke the sabbath but he also called God his own father, making himself equal to God" (Jn 5:18).

After his Resurrection, the glory of his divine Sonship became evident in his risen body. St. John writes, "we saw his glory, the glory as of the Father's only Son" (Jn 1:14).

The early Church professed its faith in the divinity of Jesus. The Council of Nicaea in 325 condemned Arius for claiming that Jesus was either just an extraordinary man or a minor divinity. "No," said Nicaea, "Jesus is the divine Son of God." The Council of Chalcedon in 451 taught that Jesus is true God and true man, "like us in all things except sin" (Heb 4:15).

These councils described the mystery of Christ as one divine person having a human and a divine nature.

Much is made today of the humanity of Christ. Yes, Jesus is definitely human. But he is also divine. It is only because he is divine that we have religious faith in him. We *remember* Plato, but we *worship* Jesus. We *revere* Lincoln, but we *adore* Christ. George Washington is dead. But Jesus is alive!

If Jesus were only human, we would simply admire him as a great teacher and possibly imitate his virtues. But because he is also divine, we believe he is alive right now and capable of saving us from evil, giving us the greatest fulfillment, and filling our hearts with unimaginable joy.

Reflection

1. *What does the name Jesus Christ mean?*
   "The name Jesus means 'God saves.' . . . '[T]here is no other name under heaven given among men by which we must be saved' (Acts 4:12).
   "The title 'Christ' means 'Anointed One' (Messiah)" (*Catechism*, 452-453).

2. *How is Jesus "Son of God"?*
   "The title 'Son of God' signifies the unique and eternal relationship of Jesus Christ to God his Father: he is the only Son of the Father (cf. Jn 1:14, 18; 3:16, 18); he is God himself (cf. Jn 1:1). To be a Christian, one must believe that Jesus Christ is the Son of God (cf. Acts 8:37; 1 Jn 2:23)" (*Catechism*, 454).

3. *Why do we speak of Jesus as "Lord"?*
   "The title 'Lord' indicates divine sovereignty. To confess or invoke Jesus as Lord is to believe in his divinity" (*Catechism*, 455).

Prayer

"[A]t the name of Jesus every knee should bend . . . and every tongue confess that Jesus Christ is Lord, to the glory of God the Father" (Phil 2:10-11). We adore you, Jesus Christ, and we praise you, for you are Lord.

Resource

Catechism, 422-455

Glossary

Chalcedon. Church council held in 451. It reaffirmed the traditional faith of the Church that Jesus was truly God and truly man. In Jesus there is one divine person wedded to a divine and a human nature.

Life Application

1. If Jesus were not the Son of God, would I still be required to have faith in him? How is my reaction to Jesus different from the way I approach Lincoln or Gandhi?
2. Which of these three images best illustrates for me the divinity of Jesus: (a) his Baptism in the Jordan, (b) his Transfiguration on Mount Tabor, or (c) his forgiveness and defense of the woman taken in adultery? What reasons governed my choice?
3. Which sacrament reminds me most that Jesus is God? Why? Why is it important to exercise my faith in Christ's divinity?

Focus

[Christ's divinity] shines forth whenever His human nature [was] humbled. . . . If He was born of a humble maid in a stable, there were angels of heaven to announce His glory; if He lowered Himself to companionship with an ox and an ass in a manger, there was a shining star to lead Gentiles to Him as King. . . . [If] He humbled Himself as a sinner to receive the baptism of John, there was a Voice from Heaven to proclaim the glory of the Eternal Son who needed no purification; if there were townspeople to reject Him and throw Him over a cliff, there was the Divine power to walk through the midst of them unharmed; if He was nailed to a Cross, there was a sun to hide its face in shame and an earth to quake in rebellion against what creatures did to its Creator; if He was laid in a tomb, there were angels to herald His Resurrection.

Archbishop Fulton J. Sheen, *Life of Christ*

Chapter 12

Conceived by the Spirit – Born of the Virgin

The Annunciation to Mary inaugurates "the fullness of time" (Gal 4:4), the time of the fulfillment of God's promises and preparations.

Catechism, 484

Archaeologists say the first humans were cave people. Christian faith tells us humanity was born again in a cave at Bethlehem. Startling contrasts meet us at the cave. The God who made the universe has hands too small to enfold the heads of the cattle. The God of infinite independence must depend on his mother's milk for survival.

If we forget the child is God, then this event is just another charming birth scene with no special meaning. If we only see the God and not the man-child, we endow the scene with magic and myth, not the history that is really there. We are encountering mystery which invites our faith. Humanists merely admire the baby. Shepherds and kings adore the incarnate God. Unbelievers rock the cradle. Believers let the cradle rock the world. We come with silence, faith, and awe.

The infancy narratives of Matthew and Luke describe how the Son of God became a man, conceived by the Holy Spirit, born of the Virgin Mary. The first chapter of John's Gospel outlines the pre-existence of the divine Word who became flesh in Jesus Christ. This is not a myth or a symbol. It is a historical event, a saving truth that lies at the heart of our faith. Scripture reveals this to us. We adore and respond in faith. In Jesus Christ, a divine person shows us a human face. We see his glory (cf. Jn 1:14).

As Son of God, Jesus is divine. As son of Mary, Jesus is human. God sent the angel Gabriel to Mary to announce that she would virginally bear a son by the power of the Spirit. Love cannot be commanded. Love on demand is force, not affection. God invited Mary to accept this great gift. Even God had to wait for an answer. In that silence, Mary gathered up her whole soul for a response.

Meditating on that moment, St. Bernard pictured the world and history waiting for a reply. Adam and Eve beg her for a yes. So also do Abraham, Moses, and David. The impatient Bernard wants her to answer quickly. "Answer with a word. Receive the Word. Speak your human word. Conceive the divine Word. Breathe a passing word. Embrace the eternal Word."

Mary understood perfectly that her response must rise from the depth of her faith life. As the answer coursed to her lips, it really came from her heart. "May it be done to me according to your word" (Lk 1:38). Later, Elizabeth praised Mary for this, "Blessed are you who believed" (Lk 1:45).

The scriptural accounts of the Incarnation confirm our belief in Christ's humanity as well as his divinity. Cardinal Newman's favorite doctrine was the Incarnation. "For the convenience of arrangement, I will consider the Incarnation, the central truth of the Gospel and the source whence we are to draw out its principles." He focused on the bright dawn of Christmas to illumine the mystery of redemption.

Christ's divinity should not blind our view of his humanity. His humanity should not make us imagine he is not divine. We can never repeat our faith in the whole Christ too often. Blessed be Jesus Christ, true God and true man.

Reflection

1. *How do we declare our faith in Jesus Christ?*
   "Jesus Christ is true God and true man, in the unity of his divine person; for this reason he is the one and only mediator between God and men.

   "Jesus Christ possesses two natures, one divine and the other human, not confused, but united in the one person of the God's Son" (*Catechism*, 480-481).

2. *How may we envision Christ's humanity?*
   "Christ, being true God and true man, has a human intellect and will, perfectly attuned and subject to his divine intellect and divine will, which he has in common with the Father and the Holy Spirit" (*Catechism*, 482).

3. *How did the Incarnation occur?*
   "Mary was invited to conceive him in whom the 'whole fullness of deity' would dwell 'bodily' (Col 2:9)."

   "Hence, the Church confesses that Mary is truly 'Mother of God' (*Theotokos*)" (*Catechism*, 484, 495).

Prayer

O come, let us adore him,
O come, let us adore him,
O come, let us adore him,
Christ the Lord.
　　　　"O Come, All Ye Faithful"

Resource

Catechism, 456-511

Glossary

Gabriel. The angel who was sent by God to ask the Virgin Mary to become the Mother of God.

Infancy Narratives. Matthew 1-2 and Luke 1-2 deal with the birth of Jesus Christ, each from a different perspective. Their accounts complement and enrich each other.

The Word. The first chapter of John's Gospel describes the pre-existence of Jesus Christ as the divine Word who fully expresses the Father and who became flesh and dwelt among us.

Life Application

1. When I think of the humanity of Jesus, I am most moved by: (a) the Christmas story; (b) Christ's Passion and death; or (c) Christ's kindness to the poor, the sinful, and the lonely. The reasons for my choice are . . .

2. Why do I find the Gospel stories about the life of Jesus so important for my faith growth? Jesus is my model and also the One who creates in me the virtue he models. Which of his virtues do I admire the most?

3. Personally, how do I keep in harmony and balance the divinity and humanity of Jesus? Why is it necessary that I do this?

Focus

For the last Christmas of his life, St. Francis of Assisi moved to a cave on a hillside opposite the town of Greccio. He and the brothers transformed the cave into a Bethlehem scene. They lined the cave with straw, installed a crib, and brought an altar for Mass.

At midnight the people of Greccio came in procession, their lanterns looking like stars streaming across the valley. They sang the ancient carols of Umbria, echoing the gloria of the angels.

Arrived at the cave, they were charmed by the scene. An ox and an ass flanked the empty crib. Mass began. At homily time Francis stood by the crib to talk about the birth of Jesus. Awe engulfed the listeners. Amid a golden light they saw Francis reach into the empty crib and lift out a baby and cradle him in his arms, saying, "Behold the Savior of the world."

After Mass, Francis disappeared. When the morning star appeared they found him absorbed in prayer, his face turned toward Bethlehem.

And that is how the custom of having a Christmas crib began.

Chapter 13

Holy Mary, Mother of God

What the Catholic faith believes about Mary is based on what it believes about Christ, and what it teaches about Mary illumines in turn its faith in Christ.

Catechism, 487

In the year 431, St. Cyril of Alexandria led a delegation of Egyptian bishops to the Council of Ephesus. Bishop John of Antioch brought a contingent of bishops from Syria. Pope Celestine I sent three legates. St. Augustine had been invited, but died before the council opened. The most famous decision of that council was to declare that Mary was the "Mother of God" (*Theotokos,* or "God-bearer").

Why were they moved to affirm the ancient faith of the Church about Mary? Because the patriarch of Constantinople, Nestorius, was teaching that the child born of Mary was only human. He argued that only after the birth, the Word of God was united with the human Jesus. Mary could not be God's mother.

The council Fathers rejected this teaching. They asserted that the Son of God was united to the humanity of Jesus from the beginning. "He made the birth of his flesh into his own flesh. Thus we do not hesitate to call the Holy Virgin: Mother of God." Of course, Mary was the mother of the whole Jesus Christ, divine and human. They were primarily making a faith statement about Jesus. Teachings about Mary shed light on Jesus. This principle applies to Mary's Immaculate Conception and perpetual virginity.

Some mistakenly think that the "Immaculate Conception" refers to Mary's begetting Jesus without sexual union with a man. But it really means that Mary was herself conceived without original sin. The Fathers of the Eastern Churches call Mary the Mother of God, "the all-holy one." They celebrate her as "free of the stain of sin," as though fashioned and formed by the Holy Spirit into a new creature. This gift of hers comes entirely from Christ and prepares her for her role as Mother of our Savior.

The Church also affirms that Jesus was conceived by the power of the Holy Spirit alone in the womb of the Virgin Mary. This has its basis in the Gospels (Mt 1:18-25; Lk 1:35). Clearly, the Gospel narratives understand this conception as a work of God that goes beyond human comprehension and capability. Some people, both ancient and modern, dismiss this as a myth or a theological construction. But only faith can see this truth and treasure it.

Further, the Church believes that Mary always remained a virgin. Here again, faith affirms what seems strange to unaided human reason. Since earliest times, the Church's liturgy acclaims Mary as "ever virgin." Some object that the Scripture mentions brothers and sisters of Jesus (Mk 3:31-35; 1 Cor 9:5; Gal 1:19). But the Church has always understood these passages as referring to the cousins of Jesus. The Council of Capua in 392, led by St. Ambrose, reaffirmed the faith of the Church in Mary's perpetual virginity. Her original virginity prepared her to be the Mother of God. Her perpetual virginity prepared her to be the Mother of the Church. On the Cross, Jesus called Mary to be the mother of the redeemed: "Woman, behold, your son" (Jn 19:26).

We love Mary because we love Jesus. We love the mother because we love the son.

Reflection

1. *Why is Mary the "Immaculate Conception"?*

   "From among the descendants of Eve, God chose the Virgin Mary to be the mother of his Son. 'Full of grace,' Mary is 'the most excellent fruit of redemption' (*Sacrosanctum Concilium*, 103): . . . she was totally preserved from the stain of original sin . . ." (*Catechism*, 508).

2. *Why can we say Mary is the Mother of God?*

   "Mary is truly 'Mother of God' since she is the mother of the eternal Son of God . . ." (*Catechism*, 509).

3. *What is the Church's faith about Mary's virginity?*

   "Mary 'remained a virgin in conceiving her Son, a virgin in giving birth to him, a virgin in carrying him, a virgin in nursing him at her breast, always a virgin' (St. Augustine, Serm. 186, 1: PL 38,999). . . .

   "The Virgin Mary 'cooperated through free faith and obedience in human salvation' (*Lumen Gentium*, 56)" (*Catechism*, 510-511).

Prayer

Hail Mary, full of grace, the Lord is with thee. Blessed art thou among women, and blessed is the fruit of thy womb, Jesus. Holy Mary, Mother of God, pray for us sinners now and at the hour of our death. Amen.

Resource

Catechism, 484-511

Glossary

Capua. Regional council of the Church in 392 led by St. Ambrose and reaffirming the faith of the Church in the perpetual virginity of Mary.

Ephesus. Council of the Church, held in 431, which reaffirmed the faith of the Church in Mary as truly the Mother of God.

Immaculate Conception. A dogma of the Church that declares Mary was free of original sin from the first moment of her conception, due to the anticipated merits of her Son.

Nestorius. He denied Mary was Mother of God, claiming that the child born of her was only human, then later made divine by God.

Life Application

1. Elizabeth blessed Mary "because she believed." Mary is my model of faith. What can I learn about my faith growth in meditating on the life of Mary? How strong do I think my faith is right now?

2. At Cana Mary interceded with Jesus on the couple's behalf. At the Cross, Jesus entrusted John to Mary, saying, "Behold, your mother." How convinced am I of Mary's powerful intercession? How do I turn to her for guidance? What more should I do?

3. Tradition says John brought Mary with him to Ephesus. Her contemplative prayer accompanied his writing of the Gospel and Paul's preaching in Ephesus. How can Mary help me to meditate each day and be more prayerful?

Focus

Since [Mary] lived in the house of the beloved disciple, it would be astonishing if the Gospel . . . had not been inspired by her presence and what she had to say. Certainly it is characteristic that the first apparition of our Lady about which we learn from trustworthy sources is the vision of . . . Gregory the Wonderworker. . . . While one night he was pondering the word of faith, a form appeared to him, an old man in the attitude and dress of a priest [St. John the Evangelist], who told him he would show him divine wisdom in order to remove his uncertainty. Then he gestured sideways with his hand and showed him another form of more than human dignity and almost unbearable splendor [the Mother of God]. This figure said to John . . . that he should expound the mystery of faith to [Gregory]. Whereupon, John said he would gladly comply with the wishes of the Mother of the Lord and explained the mystery of the Trinity to Gregory in clear words. Gregory wrote down at once what was said and later preached on this to the people. . . . It is one of the finest and clearest [expressions of the Trinity] we have.

Hans Urs von Balthasar, *Mary for Today*

Chapter 14

The Jesus of the Gospels

... the articles of faith concerning his Incarnation and Passover do shed light on the whole of his earthly life

Catechism, 512

Christmas tells us who Jesus is. Holy Week and Easter tell us why he came. The Gospels were written "that you may [come to] believe that Jesus is the Messiah, the Son of God, and that through this belief you may have life in his name" (Jn 20:31). The evangelists "selected certain of the many elements which had been handed on . . . always in such a fashion that they have told us the honest truth about Jesus" (*Dei Verbum*, 19; SVC).

The *Catechism* speaks of Christ's person and his earthly words and deeds in terms of "mystery." Christ's humanity is a sacrament of his divinity. His visible earthly life discloses the invisible mystery of his divine sonship. His parables, miracles, sermons, and wisdom sayings help us "to see our God made visible, and so we are caught up in the love of God we cannot see" (Preface for Christmas, *Sacramentary*).

Through faith we have communion in the mysteries of Christ by following his example and by living in him and welcoming him to live in us. This happens through our active participation in the sacraments, our life of prayer, our Christian behavior, our openness to the Holy Spirit, and the graces available to us.

We are enriched by the mysteries of Christ's infancy and hidden life: his birth, the circumcision, Epiphany, the flight into Egypt, his hidden life at Nazareth.

We grow in Christ by identification with the mysteries of his public life, such as his baptism, the temptation, his preaching and witnessing of the kingdom of God. In the forty days of Lent, for example, we relive the mystery of Christ in the desert.

What is the kingdom of God? It is the Father's gracious offer of a sharing in divine life, beginning here on earth and permanently in eternal life. The Father does this by gathering us into his Son in the Church. While this kingdom is never an earthly utopia, it can have practical expression in love, justice, and mercy. We enter the kingdom through faith in Christ and obedience to the divine will. Everyone is invited.

Christ's parables, Sermon on the Mount, and Last Supper Discourse were calls to salvation and kingdom living. Christ's miracles were both acts of compassion as well as signs of the divine presence, power, and kingdom. Jesus gave the apostles the authority to bring the kingdom to the world. He conferred on Peter the leadership of the apostles by giving him the "keys to the kingdom" (Mt 16:19). By Christ's will, the apostles passed this authority to the Pope and bishops.

In the mystery of the Transfiguration, we behold a foretaste of the kingdom. The Byzantine liturgy states, "You were transfigured on a mountain. Your disciples contemplated your glory, Christ God, so that when they saw you crucified, they would understand that your Passion was freely willed. They would announce to the world, you are truly the shining forth of the Father."

We do more than simply look at Jesus. Each time we behold him with faith and love, we are transformed into him.

Reflection

1. *Why is Christ's earthly life important for us?*
   " 'The whole of Christ's life was a continual teaching: his silences, his miracles, his gestures, his prayer, his love for people, his special affection for the little and the poor, his acceptance of the total sacrifice on the Cross for the redemption of the world, and his Resurrection are the actualization of his word and the fulfillment of Revelation' (Pope John Paul II, *Catechesi Tradendae*, 9)" (*Catechism*, 561).

2. *Why do we speak of the "mystery" of Christ's words and deeds?*
   " 'For this reason we, who have been made like to him, who have died with him and risen with him, are taken up into the mysteries of his life, until we reign together with him'(*Lumen Gentium*, 7)" (*Catechism*, 562).

3. *Where is Christ's kingdom?*
   " 'This kingdom shone out before men in the word, in the works, and in the presence of Christ' (*Lumen Gentium*, 5). The Church is the seed and beginning of this kingdom. Her keys are entrusted to Peter" (*Catechism*, 567).

Prayer

Thy kingdom come; thy will be done on earth as it is in heaven.

Resource

Catechism, 512-570

Glossary

Kingdom of God. The substance of Christ's preaching and witness. The kingdom of God is a divine reality of love, justice, and mercy, partially realized on earth, fully realized in heaven.

Miracles. The Gospels of Matthew, Mark, and Luke portray the miracles of Jesus as acts of compassion. John's miracle narratives are called signs which reveal the glory and saving intentions of Jesus.

Mysteries of Christ's Life. The events of Christ's life are both examples for kingdom living as well as sources of transforming grace to make that possible.

Parables. Stories told by Jesus both to illustrate a divine truth and the meaning of the kingdom, but also are challenging narratives summoning us to deeper faith.

Life Application

1. Jesus asks me to feed the hungry, give drink to the thirsty, clothe the naked, shelter the homeless, visit the sick, ransom the captive, and bury the dead. How can I do a better job in responding to these corporal works of mercy?
2. I am also called to practice the spiritual works of mercy: instruct the ignorant, counsel the doubtful, admonish the sinner, bear wrongs patiently, forgive offenses, comfort the afflicted, and pray for the living and the dead. How well am I doing in these challenges?
3. What events in the life of Jesus do I find best for my meditations?

Focus

The contemplation of Our Lord is not only holy but sanctifying; even only to think of Him, to look at Him with faith and love, sanctifies us. For certain souls, the life of Christ Jesus is one subject of meditation among many others; this is not enough. Christ is not one of the means of spiritual life. He is all our spiritual life. The Father sees all in His Word, in His Christ. Why should not Christ be equally our all, our Model, our Satisfaction, our Hope, our Substitute, our Light, our Strength, our Joy? This truth is so important that I want to insist upon it.

Abbot Columba Marmion, O.S.B.,
Christ the Life of the Soul

Chapter 15

Hold High the Cross

It is "love to the end" (Jn 13:1) that confers on Christ's sacrifice its value as redemption and reparation, as atonement and satisfaction.

Catechism, 616

According to legend, the thorn bird sings just once in its life. Leaving its nest, it searches for a bush with long, sharp thorns. Upon finding such a bush, it impales itself on the biggest thorn. At that moment it begins to sing. The bird outcarols the lark, and the world pauses to listen. God smiles with pleasure at the captivating melody. What is the message of this sacrificial music? Life's most satisfying moment can only be purchased at the price of great pain. So says the legend.

The reality of that message occurred in Christ's agony in the garden, scourging at the pillar, crowning with thorns, carrying of the Cross, crucifixion, death, and burial.

The greatest of all meditations is the Passion of Jesus Christ. Of all the words and acts of Jesus, none has the capacity to touch the heart with love and gratitude more than those that occurred during his Passion. The story of the Cross has converted hearts from apostolic times to the present. That is why the Passion narratives are the longest and most moving parts of all four Gospels.

Why else did St. Paul resolutely say, "I did not come [to you] with sublimity of words or of wisdom. For I resolved to know nothing while I was with you except Jesus Christ and him crucified" (1 Cor 2:1-2).

Christian devotion has organized reflection on the Passion into the five sorrowful mysteries of the Rosary, the fourteen Stations of the Cross, and the seven last words of Jesus. Prayerful people have taken possession of the Passion to praise God for this supreme act of divine love by which we are redeemed from all that oppresses us, above all from sin.

Who is responsible for the death of Jesus? All of us, from Adam and Eve to the present generation, who, in pride and disobedience, have sinned. It is wrong to blame the Jewish people for this, as happened in history. "Even though the Jewish authorities and those who followed their lead pressed for the death of Christ . . . neither all Jews indiscriminately at that time, nor Jews today, can be charged with the crimes committed during his Passion" (*Nostra Aetate*, 4; SVC).

The whole life of Christ was an offering to the Father for the forgiveness of our sins. John the Baptist called Jesus the Lamb of God come to take away our sins. At the Last Supper Jesus anticipated his free self-offering. In instituting the Eucharist he spoke of his body to be broken and his blood to be poured out. At Gethsemane he surrendered his will to the Father. There and on the Cross, he substituted his obedience for our disobedience.

He died a real death and was buried in a real grave. The creed says he descended into hell, that is, into the region of the just who had died. There, he opened the gates of heaven to the just ones who came before him.

At the ninth hour on Good Friday, the high priest killed the last lamb at the Temple. He said one word over the victim: "*Kalah*" ("It is finished"). At Calvary at the same moment Jesus, the Lamb of God, said his last word: "*Kalah*" ("It is finished"). Jesus completed his obedience to the Father. We hope to do the same.

Reflection

1. *Why did Christ die for us?*
    " 'Christ died for our sins in accordance with the scriptures' (1 Cor 15:3).
    "Our salvation flows from God's initiative of love for us, because 'he loved us and sent his Son to be the expiation for our sins' (1 Jn 4:10)" (*Catechism*, 619-620).

2. *What was the meaning of Christ's obedience?*
    "By his loving obedience to the Father, 'unto death, even death on a cross' (Phil 2:8), Jesus fulfills the atoning mission (cf. Isa 53:10) of the suffering Servant, who will 'make many righteous; and he shall bear their iniquities' (Isa 53:11; cf. Rom 5:19)" (*Catechism*, 623).

3. *What does "descent into hell" mean?*
    "Scripture calls the abode of the dead, to which the dead Christ went down, 'hell' — *Sheol* in Hebrew or *Hades* in Greek — because those who are there are deprived of the vision of God."
    "He opened heaven's gates for the just who had gone before him" (*Catechism*, 633, 637).

Prayer

Father, by the suffering and death of your only Son, Jesus Christ, make us pleasing to you. Alone we can do nothing, but may his perfect sacrifice win us your mercy and love.

Resource

Catechism, 571-637

Glossary

Passion. From the Latin word for suffering. It refers here to the redemptive suffering and death of Jesus.

Rosary. A prayer said with beads. Each set of an Our Father, ten Hail Marys, and a Glory Be to the Father is accompanied by a meditation on a mystery of Christ.

Sacrifice. The offering of a victim to a god on behalf of a people. The Son of God became this victim, a living Lamb of God, to redeem us from our sins.

Life Application

1. How can the sufferings and death of Jesus help me to make sense of my own pain and of others whom I know? How have I approached tragedies which have touched my life and family?
2. Jesus taught that being his disciple means: Lose the self. Take the cross. Follow him. What would I need to change in order to follow each of these three steps more faithfully?
3. Jesus suffered and died to save me from my sins. In what areas of my life do I need conversion from sinfulness? How can the Jesus of the Passion help me?

Focus

Polish photographer Adam Bujak and American journalist Marjorie Young have published a book with pictures and text, *Journeys to Glory.* The topic deals with the rural rituals of Catholic Poland. Their third photo-essay is "The Celebration of the Sufferings of Our Lord." It takes place in a tiny town deep in rural Poland. One hundred-fifty-thousand pilgrims are there for Holy Week. Marjorie Young writes:

> They gather around a life-sized wooden statue of Jesus, whose hands are chained to a pole and on whose body wound marks can be seen. The statue portrays Jesus, not as an elegant figure, but as a simple peasant. Pilgrims place candles around him and talk to him as a friend. They stroke his face lovingly and tell him their problems. Some ask for cures or to be able to see or hear better. Others kiss his hands and his face and prostrate themselves before him.

Chapter 16

The Glory of Easter

"Christ has risen from the dead!
Dying, he conquered death;
To the dead, he has given life"
(Troparion of Easter of the Byzantine liturgy).

Catechism, 638

Most people like happy endings to a story. Sometimes they change the classics for this purpose. In the eighteenth century, Shakespeare's tragedy of King Lear was changed so that Lear was restored to the throne. Easter is more than a contrived ending.

Christ's Resurrection was not tacked onto the Passion like a pleasant addition. The risen Jesus wears the marks of the Passion. The death and Resurrection of Jesus were more than the result of random historical forces, but part of an eternal plan of salvation. Christians view the life, death, and Resurrection of Jesus as the world's greatest drama. God is the author of the drama. The Gospel is not a tragedy, but a narrative with a true happy ending, consistent with the life and death of Jesus.

John's Gospel makes this abundantly clear. Easter so illumines the suffering that went before it that the very Cross itself is a pool of light. The liturgy of the Eastern Church sings, "Since it brings life, the tomb of Jesus is lovelier than paradise. It is the fountain from which our resurrection springs." John's Gospel is so full of Easter joy that it contains two chapters about the event. Christ's Resurrection is both a true historical happening as well as a transcendent event and mystery.

St. Paul speaks of the *living Tradition* of the resurrection that he discovered after his conversion on the Damascus road (1 Cor 15:3-4). Paul insists that the twelve apostles and more than five hundred others witnessed the reality of the risen Jesus. His resurrected body was different from that of Lazarus, Jairus' daughter, and the young man of Naim. Their bodies returned to an earthly existence and died again. Christ's risen body is filled with the power of the Spirit. It shares the divine life in its state of glory. Paul calls him the *heavenly man* (1 Cor 15:47).

The Resurrection is historical, but it also transcends history. It remains at the heart of the mystery of faith. The Resurrection is a truth of faith. It is a transcendent intervention of God in history. It is both a challenge to and a confirmation of our faith. "[I]f Christ has not been raised, then empty [too] is our preaching; empty, too, your faith" (1 Cor 15:14).

The Resurrection makes credible everything Jesus did and taught. Easter opens up the glory of Christ's divinity. Christmas and Easter form one bond, revealing to us the accomplishment of the eternal plan of God for our salvation. By his death Jesus freed us from sin. By his Resurrection, he opens for us the path to new life. Finally, the risen Jesus is the principle and source of our own future resurrection. "For just as in Adam all die, so too in Christ shall all be brought to life" (1 Cor 15:22).

Easter helps us taste the heavenly gift and the powers of the age to come (Heb 6:4-5). Every year, Easter faith takes on the bright sound of a trumpet blast. What does it sing? Everything belongs to you, whether it be the world, or life or death, or the present or the future. All belong to you, and you to Christ, and Christ to God (see 1 Cor 3:23-24).

Reflection

1. *What is the history and mystery of Christ's Resurrection?*
    "Faith in the Resurrection has as its object an event which is historically attested to by the disciples, who really encountered the Risen One. At the same time, this event is mysteriously transcendent insofar as it is the entry of Christ's humanity into the glory of God" (*Catechism*, 656).

2. *What does the empty tomb tell us?*
    "The empty tomb and the linen cloths lying there signify in themselves that by God's power Christ's body had escaped the bonds of death and corruption. They prepared the disciples to encounter the Risen Lord" (*Catechism*, 657).

3. *What does Christ's Resurrection mean for us?*
    "Christ, 'the first-born from the dead' (Col 1:18), is the principle of our own resurrection, even now by the justification of our souls (cf. Rom 6:4), and one day by the new life he will impart to our bodies (cf. Rom 8:11)" (*Catechism*, 658).

Prayer

O Christ of glory, I renew my faith in your Resurrection from the dead. I praise you for the salvation you have brought me. I believe in the future resurrection of my body.

Resource

Catechism, 638-658

Glossary

Empty Tomb. Signifies that Jesus' body escaped the bonds of death.

Resurrection. Refers to the rising of Christ's body from the dead to the life of glory. It was a historical event, but it also transcends history as a mystery of faith.

Life Application

1. Why is the Resurrection of Jesus an essential part of his saving us from sin? What is there about Easter that fills me with joy? How can I be an "alleluia" from head to toe?

2. My body seeks pleasure. My soul looks for happiness. My deep inner spirit yearns for absolute joy. In what way does the Resurrection of Jesus respond to these desires in the most satisfying manner?

3. Which of these Easter stories inspires me most deeply: Christ revealing himself to Mary Magdalene in the garden? Jesus helping Thomas overcome his doubt? Jesus calling Peter to "Feed my lambs" after Peter's triple affirmation of love? What are the reasons for my choice?

Focus

As [the newly baptized] emerge from the grace-giving womb of the font, a blaze of candles burns brightly beneath the tree of faith. The Easter festival brings the grace of holiness from heaven to [us]. Through the repeated celebration of the sacred mysteries [we] receive the spiritual nourishment of the sacraments. Fostered at the very heart of holy Church, the fellowship of one community worships the one God, adoring the triple name of his essential holiness. . . .

Jesus . . . the author of life . . . brings the sunrise and the beginning of life. . . . [W]hoever follows Christ in all things will come . . . to the throne of eternal light.

Easter Homily by an Ancient Author
in the *Liturgy of the Hours*

Chapter 17

The Second Coming of Jesus

Full right to pass definitive judgment on the works and hearts of men belongs to [Christ] as redeemer of the world.

Catechism, 679

What would happen if a Pope had a vision that the end of the world was about to happen?

Novelist Morris West addressed that question in his story *The Clowns of God*. God calls the fictional Pope Gregory XVII to proclaim the last days near the year 2000. He writes an encyclical, *In These Last Fateful Years of the Millennium*.

The college of cardinals convened and judged this would be too traumatic for the world. They opposed publishing his encyclical and advised him to resign. If he refused, they would declare him mentally incompetent and force his abdication. The Pope voluntarily resigned and retired to a monastery. The story continues against a background of nuclear threats and superpower rivalry. For those who will read the novel, I will not spoil it by revealing the ending.

When will Jesus come again?

Jesus Christ ascended into heaven forty days after his Resurrection. His Resurrection and Ascension reveal him as Lord of heaven and earth as well as all of history. The Father has "put all things beneath his feet and gave him as head over all things to the church, which is his body" (Eph 1:22-23). Though he is in heaven, he is also on earth in the Church through the redemption of each of us and in the world at large by the power of the Holy Spirit.

History has entered its final phase. We are already in the "last days." "Children, it is the last hour" (1 Jn 2:18). We have no knowledge how long these days will last. Jesus calls us to proclaim the mystery of his salvation and to make present as much as we can the reality of his kingdom of love, justice, and mercy. Our witness in word and deed should invite all to faith in the person and message of Jesus Christ.

We believe this world will end some day and that Jesus will come to judge the living and the dead. Can we know the date? No. "But of that day or hour no one knows, neither the angels in heaven, nor the Son, but only the Father" (Mk 13:32). Certain Christian sects claim to know the date and the exact historical and political circumstances that will accompany the end of time and the Second Coming. They have always been wrong and always will be.

The Church listens to Christ's teaching that it is useless to speculate about timing. What is important is to see earthly trials, tragedies, and persecutions as opportunities for faith growth and trust in God. The last book of the Bible, the Apocalypse, teaches us that God cares for us no matter how difficult circumstances become. God's love will prevail.

A surge of evil will mark the end times. But Jesus will come to defeat evil and judge all. The Father "has given all judgment to his Son" (Jn 5:22). We are tempted to say we live in the worst of times. But other ages of history thought the same. Our calling is positive. Live in hope despite all appearances. Trust in the power of Jesus Christ as Lord.

Reflection

1. *What is the spiritual message of the Ascension?*
   "Christ the Lord already reigns through the Church, but all the things of this world are not yet subjected to him" (*Catechism*, 680).

2. *Is it possible to know the date of the end of the world?*
   "Since the Ascension Christ's coming in glory has been imminent, even though 'it is not for you to know times or seasons which the Father has fixed by his own authority' (Acts 1:7)" (*Catechism*, 673).

3. *What will happen on Judgment Day?*
   "On Judgment Day at the end of the world, Christ will come in glory to achieve the definitive triumph of good over evil. . . .
   "When he comes at the end of time to judge the living and the dead, the glorious Christ will reveal the secret disposition of hearts and will render to each man according to his works and according to his acceptance or refusal of grace" (*Catechism*, 681-682).

Prayer

O Christ of glory, merciful judge, rule our hearts now that we may come to the judgment with hope and love rather than with fear and trembling. Lead us to witness your salvation and kingdom now that we may participate in your glory at the end of time.

Resource

Catechism, 659-682

Glossary

Apocalypse. Title of last book of the Bible. This book is also called *Revelation*. Apocalypse means "revelation."

Ascension. Refers to Christ's ascending into heaven forty days after Easter.

Judgment Day. Will happen at the end of history when Jesus comes to bring the final victory over evil and judge the living and the dead.

Life Application

1. If I thought the world would come to an end in three years, what effect would that have on my life? What would I do about my property? Would I continue living less morally or more morally? Would I give up dieting, exercise, and other efforts to stay in good health?
2. When I see news items about sects setting dates about the world's end, what do I think about them and their prophecies? Why is Christ's teaching, "You know not the day or the hour," the most sensible way to deal with the end of time?
3. When I come before God's judgment seat, how do I think I will fare? Will God judge me more mercifully than I would evaluate myself? Will God judge me as I have judged others?

Focus

[Jesus] is coming who is everywhere present and pervades all things; he is coming to achieve in you his work of universal salvation. He is coming who came to call to repentance not the righteous but sinners. . . . Do not be afraid.

Receive him with open outstretched hands, for it was on his own hands that he sketched you. Receive him who laid your foundations on the palms of his hands. Receive him, for he took upon himself all that belongs to us except sin. . . . Glorify him for his mercy. . . .

St. Andrew of Crete in the *Liturgy of the Hours*

Chapter 18

The Spirit Is Our Dynamo

The Holy Spirit is at work with the Father and the Son from the beginning to the completion of the plan for our salvation.

Catechism, 686

Religion works best when it recovers its contact with the Holy Spirit. Then believers become doers of the Word because they are hearers of the Spirit. They act with *enthusiasm*, a word that means "the God within." Pope John Paul II has noted the power of the Spirit over our inner lives. "Under the influence of the Holy Spirit, the inner, spiritual person grows strong" (*Lord and Giver of Life*, 58).

Parishes and schools, engaged in building communities of faith, do not work alone. The generous energy from the Holy Spirit lightens their burden. Missionaries, too, are gaining their second wind from the Spirit, God's "mighty breath."

The Spirit reinforces the quest to be truly human. The Acts of the Apostles witness this. The people in Acts sing in jail, eat a hearty meal, generously share their belongings, tenderly care for and heal the sick, take up collections for the poor, passionately debate religion, write numerous letters, devise cloak-and-dagger escapes, take perilous boat rides, and pray with simplicity and fervor. It is a very human community — and also very divine — because, as they will tell you, the Spirit fills their lives.

The First Council of Constantinople in 381 declared that the Holy Spirit is God, the third person of the blessed Trinity. That was always the faith of the Church, but because Arians denied the Spirit's divinity, the council reaffirmed the Spirit's Godhead.

The Spirit fires up our faith. The Spirit enables us to say that Jesus is Lord, that is, God (1 Cor 12:3). The Spirit moves our hearts to address the first person of the Trinity as Father (Gal 4:6). The best way to keep our faith alive and growing is to be in constant communion with the Spirit.

The Church reveals the Spirit's presence in the Holy Scriptures, in the sacraments, in the Tradition of the Church Fathers, and in the witness of the saints, especially the martyrs. The Spirit is tied to the dynamism of the Church, because the Spirit is always associated with "sending" or "mission." Static persons do not move. Dynamic ones are sent and missioned.

The Father sends the Word and the Spirit for our salvation. The Son is the Word of the Father, but it is the breath (Spirit) of the Father who is active in the Word. What the Spirit did in Jesus, he will do in us. The Spirit sends us, gives us that religious "push" we need to accomplish God's will.

Because the Spirit is a divine mystery, many images are needed to appreciate his reality and action. Scripture links the Spirit with the waters of Baptism, the oil of anointing in Confirmation, the fire of religious energies, the shining cloud and fire of God's glory-presence, the seal of salvation, the hand of God's protection, the finger of exorcism driving evil from us, and the dove of peace.

The whole experience of the Spirit is one of gift. Let us thank God for this gift of holy enthusiasm and sacred power.

Reflection

1. *What is our essential belief about the Holy Spirit?*

   "To believe in the Holy Spirit is to profess that the Holy Spirit is one of the persons of the Holy Trinity, consubstantial with the Father and the Son: 'with the Father and the Son he is worshipped and glorified' " (*Catechism*, 685).

2. *Where does the Church show us the Spirit?*

   "The Church . . . is the place where we know the Holy Spirit: in the Scriptures . . . in the Tradition . . . in the Church's Magisterium . . . in the sacramental liturgy . . . in prayer . . . in the charisms and ministries by which the Church is built up . . . in the signs of apostolic and missionary life . . . in the witness of saints" (*Catechism*, 688).

3. *What images reveal the mystery of the Spirit?*

   The Spirit's reality is imaged in baptismal water, Confirmation oil/anointing, fire, cloud and light, the seal, the hand, the finger, and the dove. No one image exhausts the Spirit's infinite mystery (cf. *Catechism*, 694-701).

Prayer

Come, Holy Spirit! Make us dynamic missionaries for the Good News of Jesus Christ. Give us the courage to witness Christ's moral and spiritual teachings. Fire up our faith!

Resource

Catechism, 683-701

Glossary

Arians. Group that denied divinity of the Spirit. Refuted at First Council of Constantinople in 381.

Consubstantial. Literally means "with the same substance." Refers here to our faith that the Spirit has the same divine nature as the Father and the Son.

Holy Spirit. The third person of the blessed Trinity. Works with the Father and the Son to complete our salvation.

Life Application

1. Daily meditation and silent prayer help me to be attentive to the vastness of my inner life, a world as great as the world outside me. My faith in the Holy Spirit grows when my awareness of my inner, spiritual nature advances. How much time do I give each day to growing attentiveness to my inner world? Do I dwell on the truth that I am a temple of the Spirit?

2. What means do I use to be more spiritual and less materialistic? What more should I do? What prayers do I use to keep me in touch with the Spirit?

3. How can my relation to the Spirit assist me to overcome the tendencies to pride, anger, lust, greed, envy, excess, and laziness?

Focus

The Spirit comes gently and makes himself known by his fragrance. He is not felt as a burden, for he is light. . . . Rays of light and knowledge stream before him as he approaches. The Spirit comes with a tenderness of a true friend and protector to save, to heal, to teach, to counsel, to strengthen, to console. The Spirit comes to enlighten [our] mind . . . and through [us], the minds of others. . . .

As light strikes the eyes of [one] who comes out of darkness into the sunshine and enables him to see clearly things he could not discern before, so light [of the Spirit] floods [our souls] and enables [us] to see clearly things . . . beyond the range of human vision, things hitherto undreamed of.

St. Cyril of Jerusalem in the *Liturgy of the Hours*

Chapter 19

Scripture Tells the Holy Spirit's Story

The prophetic texts that directly concern the sending of the Holy Spirit are oracles by which God speaks to the heart. . . .

Catechism, 715

In the ancient Jewish liturgy, Pentecost was the feast of Mount Sinai. It celebrated the giving of the Ten Commandments to Moses and the sealing of God's covenant with his people. A mighty wind and fire swept the slopes of Sinai, evoking awe. The wind was the breath/Spirit of God as the source of life. The fire was God's glory, manifesting his presence to his people.

The Upper Room of the Christian Pentecost is the new Sinai. Once again the mighty breath/Spirit of God and his fiery presence sweeps through the human community. Pentecost is a new Sinai in which the Spirit is set as a seal on the universe, a declaration of God's irrevocable love for all people.

Scripture reveals the work of the Spirit in the entire work of creation and redemption. "It is appropriate that the Holy Spirit should reign over, sanctify, and animate creation, for he is God and consubstantial with the Father and the Son. To him is due all power over life, for he guards creation in the Father through the Son" (Troparia of the Byzantine matins of the Sunday of the second mode).

The work of the Spirit is present, though hidden in signs and images, in all the key moments of the Old Testament. We behold the Spirit's involvement in the call of Abraham and as the cloud and fire associated with the call of Moses and the giving of the Law. The Spirit anoints judges and the kings and speaks through the prophets. After the exile, the Spirit prompts the expectation of the Messiah. The gifts of the Spirit will dwell in the Messiah. The Spirit will lead the Messiah to be the historic fulfillment of the redemptive, Suffering Servant (cf. Isa 53). The Spirit will arouse and inspire the community of the poor (the *anawim*), the holy remnant who prepare for the Messiah.

In the New Testament the Spirit's work becomes visible, overshadowing Mary at the Annunciation, giving force and energy to the ministry of John the Baptist, and powerfully linked to the life, death, and Resurrection of Jesus.

In Mary, the Spirit realizes the saving plan of the Father through the birth of the Father's Son and creates a community of all the devout poor who come to Christ: the shepherds, the magi, Simeon and Anna, the Cana couple, and the first disciples.

When his hour had come to be glorified, Jesus promised the gift of the Holy Spirit. Jesus explained that the Spirit will dwell in us, make clear the full meaning of his teaching, and lead us into all truth. As for our sinfulness, the Spirit will convince us of it, convict us of our evil, and convert our hearts to Christ and the gift of grace.

On Easter night, Jesus breathed on his apostles the gift of the Spirit (Jn 20:22). This is sometimes called the "Johannine Pentecost." It anticipates the full public gift of the Spirit that is described in St. Luke's account of Pentecost (Acts 2).

Christians should be souls on fire. We will be warm as long as we stay near the Spirit of divine fire. An old hymn says, "What a friend we have in Jesus." It is just as true to sing, "What a friend we have in the Holy Spirit!"

Reflection

1. *What are the hidden works of the Spirit in the Old Testament?*
   Through signs and images we perceive the work of the Spirit in creation, the calls of Abraham and Moses, the anointing of judges and kings, the inspiration of the prophets, the promise and expectation of the Messiah (cf. *Catechism* 703-715).

2. *What are the great public acts of the Spirit in the Gospels?*
   The Gospels manifest the Spirit's dramatic presence in the Annunciation to Mary, the ministry of John the Baptist, and the life, death, and Resurrection of Jesus Christ (cf. *Catechism*, 717-730).

3. *What are the two accounts of the giving of the Spirit?*
   John 20 narrates how Jesus breathes on the apostles on Easter night, giving them the Spirit. Acts 2 tells us of the public and definitive gift of the Spirit to the Church (cf. *Catechism*, 730-731).

Prayer

Come, Holy Spirit, lead us into truth. Unite us with Jesus. Help us prefer grace to sin. Fill us with divine life and love. Make us courageous witnesses of the Gospel.

Resource

Catechism, 702-730

Glossary

Anawim. Hebrew word for "the poor, the little ones, the humble." Specifically refers to the "faithful remnant" of holy ones who kept the ancient faith and were ready to receive the Messiah/Jesus when he came.

Pentecost. Name of Old Testament feast commemorating the giving of the covenant and Ten Commandments at Mount Sinai. Now it is the name of the Christian feast recalling the giving of the Holy Spirit to the apostles, disciples, and Mary fifty days after Easter.

Life Application

1. In the Old Testament the Spirit was active, but hidden. In the New Testament the Spirit "goes public" and his action is vividly noted. In my life is the Spirit's presence and action hidden, evident, or not noticed at all? How will I get in touch with the Spirit's dynamic presence in me?
2. When the Spirit is active in a person, there is a greater willingness to share faith. How much do I share my faith in Christ with others? How strong am I in my beliefs?
3. How enthusiastic am I about making this a better world for others? Enthusiasm comes from a Greek word meaning "the god within." What will I do to get in touch with "the Spirit within" so I can have more spiritual enthusiasm?

Focus

The whole body of the faithful who have the anointing that comes from the holy one . . . cannot err in matters of belief. This characteristic is shown in the supernatural appreciation of the faith (*sensus fidei*) of the whole people, when "from the bishops to the last of the faithful" they manifest a universal consent in matters of faith and morals. By this appreciation of the faith, aroused and sustained by the Spirit of truth, the people of God, guided by the sacred teaching authority (*magisterium*), and obeying it, receives not the mere word of men, but truly the word of God . . . the faith once for all delivered to the saints. . . . The People unfailingly adheres to this faith, penetrates it more deeply with right judgment, and applies it more fully in daily life.

Dogmatic Constitution on the Church, 12; SVC

Chapter 20

The Spirit Gives Birth to the Church

The mission of Christ and the Holy Spirit is brought to completion in the Church, which is the Body of Christ and the Temple of the Holy Spirit.

Catechism, 737

The Acts of the Apostles tell us how the Spirit created the Church. The experience of the Spirit is central to whatever happens, be that the organizing of the Church, knowing what community means, or sending forth missionaries.

The Spirit gives people a religious experience of God. Moderns think of this in terms of how they feel when they have one. But in Acts, ecstasy and interior exaltation is not the point. Acts never comments on feeling at all. People experience the Spirit in wind and fire. They do not sit around enjoying the God-feeling. Instead they proceed directly from experiencing the Spirit to preaching, healing, exorcising, building community, loving, teaching, prophesying, speaking in tongues, and dying for their belief in Christ.

The experience of the Spirit's love gives them the boldness to speak up before kings and charm an empire to come to Christ. The presence of the Spirit moves them to form community that makes present on earth the intimate communion of the Trinity. The experience of the Spirit's wisdom gives them the words they need to witness the impact of Christ's salvation on their lives. They live in community, break the Bread of Eucharist, share their goods with one another, and show charity to the poor.

The experience of the Spirit's gift of understanding motivates them to organize their community into a structured Church. This is best seen in the missionary churches established by Paul and by the institutional guidelines enunciated in the pastoral epistles to Timothy and Titus. The Spirit taught them how to provide stability and continuity for the Church. They were experiencing the Spirit, so the mystery of Christ, the Church, and the Eucharist were very real to them. These were not abstractions. They were more real than the transitory world around them.

Their experience of the Spirit filled them with "love, joy, peace, patience, kindness, gentleness, faithfulness, gentleness, [and] self control" (Gal 5:22-23). Moderns want to keep God out of the picture lest he upset probability curves, balances of power, and the integrity of human learning. New Testament people found the Spirit's presence as natural as air, water, and sun. They did not worry that he would interfere in the process of human maturing. Quite the opposite.

There have been many ages and cultures in the Church's history where the Spirit touched human awareness and the people developed very well indeed. Arts flourished, agriculture developed, cottage industries grew, intellectual life stirred, and the groundwork for modern science was established.

The Church began in the Upper Room with nine days of prayer for the coming of the Spirit. Today we need thousands of new Upper Room experiences. We need a huge prayer effort to beg the onrush of the Spirit into our world. We will need more than nine days. We need to pray in homes, churches, prisons, airplanes, statehouses, malls, before our computers, and on the freeways. Jesus said that if we pray for the Spirit, the Spirit will come. That prayer is always answered.

Reflection

1. *When does the Spirit constitute the Church?*
   "By his coming, which never ceases, the Holy Spirit causes the world to enter into the 'last days,' the time of the Church, the Kingdom already inherited though not yet consummated" (*Catechism*, 732).

2. *How does the Spirit lead us to holiness?*
   "Because the Holy Spirit is the anointing of Christ, it is Christ who, as the head of the Body, pours out the Spirit among his members to nourish, heal, and organize them in their mutual functions, to give them life, send them to bear witness, and associate them to his self-offering to the Father and to his intercession for the whole world. Through the Church's sacraments, Christ communicates his Holy and sanctifying Spirit to the members of his Body" (*Catechism*, 739).

3. *What is the greatest gift of the Holy Spirit?*
   " 'God is love' (1 Jn 4:8, 16) and love is his first gift, containing all others. 'God's love has been poured into our hearts through the Holy Spirit who has been given to us' (Rom 5:5)" (*Catechism*, 733).

Prayer

Come, Spirit, true light and eternal life.
Come, hidden mystery. Come to awake the sleepers.
Come, my joy and my glory.

St. Simeon the New Theologian

Resource

Catechism, 731-747

Glossary

Breaking of the Bread. Name given to the celebration of the Holy Eucharist in the first Christian communities.

Upper Room. In biblical times people often built a room on the roof of their one-story homes. These upper rooms were mostly used for storage, but sometimes set aside for meeting places. In the New Testament the Last Supper and Pentecost occurred in just such an upper room.

Life Application

1. The Spirit created the Church at Pentecost. Nine days of prayer preceded the event. This is the scriptural model for Church birth and growth. My home is a domestic church. How closely does prayer and my home coincide?

2. For the growth and depth of my parish Church, a great deal of personal prayer is needed from parishioners to supplement the formal services offered. What am I doing to make this possible? What could I be doing to further this goal?

3. What are evidences of the work of the Spirit in my parish community? What other impacts of the Spirit would I like to see?

Focus

On the evening of October 10, 1962, Pope John XXIII stood on the balcony of St. Peter's Basilica, overlooking the square. Three hundred thousand people packed into the piazza. Bearing candles and singing the hymns of all nations, they came to honor the vigil of the feast of Mary as Mother of God (now celebrated on January 1). They also came to celebrate the opening of the Second Vatican Council.

With his irrepressible smile, John beamed at the throng. Expansively, he said to them, "I hear you. Mary hears you. Christ hears you. You have come to open the Council. You, the People of God. You appear before me like a new Pentecost."

The year the council ended, 1965, secular magazines featured cover stories on the "death of God."

How wrong they were!

The cover story of Vatican II featured the Holy Spirit very much alive and ready to make new saints and a renewed Church.

Chapter 21

Why Do We Speak of the Church as 'Mystery'?

The Greek word *mysterion* was translated into Latin by two terms: *mysterium* and *sacramentum*. In later usage the term *sacramentum* emphasizes the visible sign of the hidden reality of salvation which was indicated by the term *mysterium*. In this sense, Christ himself is the mystery of salvation. . . .

Catechism, 774

Some years ago, CBS televised a one-hour documentary entitled, "The American Catholic Dilemma." The cultivated Italian writer Luigi Barzini narrated the show. As the documentary opened, the camera caught a coffin being lowered into a grave. As the box hovered between earth and sky, Barzini commented, "The true tension in the Catholic Church is not between liberals and conservatives, but between life and death." Situated between this life and the next, the Church ministers to the living, the dying, and the transition to life eternal.

This small image is but one way to sense the mystery of the Church. Why do we speak of the Church as mystery?

First, because the Church has a divine founder. The Father intended the existence of the Church as the sign and cause of salvation. The Son of God, Jesus Christ, instituted the Church. "For it was from the side of Christ as he slept the sleep of death on the cross, that there came forth the wondrous sacrament of the whole Church" (*Sacrosanctum Concilium*, 5; SVC). The Holy Spirit visibly manifested the Church at Pentecost.

Second, because the Holy Spirit is the enduring, cohesive force maintaining the stability and continuity of the Church. Neither human determination nor any kind of force does this; only the power of the Spirit. This happens whether historical and sociological forces are favorable or unfavorable.

The Spirit indeed works through human processes, but is not bound by them. Sound biblical scholarship shows us how the Spirit shaped the Church into a unity. The Spirit unified John's community of Love, Paul's community of Charisms at Corinth, and Timothy's community of Institution into the One Body of Christ.

Despite Roman persecution, the Dark Ages, the Black Plague, anti-popes, the Eastern Schism, the Reformation, the Enlightenment, the Kulturkampf, the hostile engine of Communism, wars, earthquakes, interior sinfulness, and exterior opposition, the Spirit, strongly and gently, sustains the existence of the Church through the centuries.

No human explanation can account for this. Only religious faith can perceive the divine Trinitarian plan at work in the remarkable history of the Church. Small wonder we have no other word to explain this but "mystery," the Church as the visible manifestation of God's saving work in history.

The lives of the saints and millions of quietly devout Catholics are yet another testimony to the mystery of the Church. These "miracles of grace" have abounded in every age of the Church, especially in its most desperate hours. The reign or kingdom of God most clearly appears in them.

Mystery here does not mean hiding something, but revealing the saving love of God and making his power effective in our lives when we respond in faith.

Reflection

1. *How do we speak of the Church as "mystery"?*
   "The Church is both visible and spiritual, a hierarchical society and the Mystical Body of Christ. She is one, yet formed of two components, human and divine. That is her mystery, which only faith can accept" (*Catechism*, 779).

2. *How is the Church a "sacrament"?*
   "The Church in this world is the sacrament of salvation, the sign and the instrument of the communion of God and men" (*Catechism*, 780).

3. *What does the word "Church" mean?*
   "The word 'Church' means 'convocation.' It designates the assembly of those whom God's Word 'convokes,' i.e., gathers together to form the People of God, and who themselves, nourished with the Body of Christ, become the Body of Christ" (*Catechism*, 777).

Prayer

We praise you, Father, for planning for the Church. We adore you, Jesus, from whose pierced side the Church was born. We worship you, Holy Spirit, for manifesting and sustaining the Church.

Resource

Catechism, 748-780

Glossary

Church. New Testament writers used the Greek word *ekklesia* for Church. They used this word to translate the Old Testament word *qahal* which meant "an assembly called by God to hear his word, offer worship, and form a covenant community with him and each other." The Greek word *ekklesia* became the Latin *ecclesia*, Italian *chiesa*, Spanish *iglesia*, and French *église*. In German it became *kirche*, translated to *kirk* in Scotland, and finally *church* in English.

Life Application

1. What do I think of the state of our Church today? From what I know of Church history, are we better off or in a worse state than in times past? What evidence do I have that "the gates of hell shall not prevail against the Church"?

2. What do I think would improve the inner life of the Church today? How can the *Catechism* help the Church become a stronger witness to Christ in the modern world?

3. Why is the Church called a "mystery"? Why do we say the Church is a Sacrament of Salvation and not just a pointer to where salvation can be found?

Focus

There is not, and there never was on earth, a work of human policy so well deserving of examination as the Roman Catholic Church. No other institution is left standing which carries the mind back to the times when the smoke of sacrifice rose from the Pantheon. . . . The proudest royal houses are but of yesterday compared with the line of Supreme Pontiffs. . . . The republic of Venice . . . was modern when compared with the Papacy. . . . The Papacy remains not in decay, . . . but full of life and vigor.

[The Church] saw the commencement of all the governments and of all the ecclesiastical establishments that now exist. . . . [We] feel no assurance that she is not destined to see the end of them all. She was great and respected before the Saxon had set foot on Britain, before the Frank had passed the Rhine, when Grecian eloquence still flourished in Antioch. . . . And she may still exist . . . when some traveler from New Zealand shall, in the midst of a vast solitude, take his stand on a broken arch of London Bridge to sketch the ruins of St. Paul's.

Thomas Babington MacCaulay in *The Faith of Millions*

Chapter 22

How Is the Church the People of God?

One becomes a *member* of this people not by a physical birth, but by being "born anew," a birth "of water and the Spirit," that is, by faith in Christ, and Baptism.

Catechism, 782

Pope John Paul II's first visit to Poland after his election was like a parish picnic on a grand scale. Millions converged on him: grandmothers in bandannas, babies held up for blessings, excited teenagers, coal miners — all roaring out the mighty hymn *Christus Vincit* ("Christ conquers").

The Pope made them feel like God's people. He let them know how much he missed them and his country. He led them in a heart-melting ballad, "Don't you miss your country, your fields and pastures, your valleys and streams?" As the people wept and sang with the Pope, they knew he was singing of a man called away to duty in Rome. He conveyed a sense of community.

People of God is a major image of the Church. The word "Church" comes from the Hebrew *qahal*, which means "called community." Who does the calling? God. Whom has he called? First, he called the people of Israel. Today God calls the Church. The Church is a community of God's people because God has convoked us and given us our divine identity.

The Church exists as long as God calls it into existence and the members respond with the "yes" of faith in Jesus Christ and live under the guidance of the Spirit. Therefore, the term "People of God" corresponds to a resolutely divine reality.

Hence the Church does not exist because of the consent of the governed and should not be equated with any political reality. We did not create the Church. God did.

Our sense of community is illustrated by the mutual sharing of the gifts of the Spirit (cf. 1 Cor 12-14).

By faith and Baptism we are initiated into the Church and become a *priestly* people offering spiritual sacrifices which Jesus makes acceptable to God. We become a *prophetic* people witnessing Christ in faith and good works. We become a *kingly* people overcoming sin, reverencing nature, and seeking the common good.

At the same time, the Church possesses a hierarchical reality because of the will of Christ. The Sacrament of Holy Orders produces a ministerial priesthood that is different in essence, not just in degree, from the common priesthood of the faithful. The ministerial priesthood is designed to serve the sanctification, guidance, and instructional needs of the priesthood of the faithful.

The ministerial priesthood is ordered to the sanctification of the priesthood of the faithful. In turn the priesthood of the faithful is ordered to the sanctification of the world.

This is an example of the harmony of the divine plan of salvation. This is why the Church is a divinely called community with clear roles and responsibilities all working together to build up the Body of Christ in the world. The first community is the Trinity. The Church, aided by the Spirit, seeks to make the love of that divine community present on earth.

Reflection

1. *Why did God call a people into existence?*

   "[God] has . . . willed to make men holy and save them, not as individuals without any bond or link between them, but rather to make them into a people who might acknowledge him and serve him in holiness" (*Catechism*, 781).

2. *How is the Church a special people?*

   The Church is a "people of God," born into it by faith and baptism, whose head is Jesus Christ, whose condition is that of children of God, whose law is to love as Christ has loved, whose mission is to be the light of the world, whose destiny is the reign of God, begun on earth and fulfilled in heaven (cf. *Catechism*, 782).

3. *What are three duties of God's people?*

   "On entering the People of God through faith and Baptism, one receives a share in this people's unique, *priestly* vocation. . . .

   " 'The holy People of God shares also in Christ's *prophetic* office. . . .'

   "Finally, the People of God shares in the *royal* office of Christ. . . . For the Christian, 'to reign is to serve him,' particularly when serving 'the poor and the suffering, in whom the Church recognizes the image of her poor and suffering founder' (*Lumen Gentium*, 8)" (*Catechism*, 784-786).

Prayer

Father, we are your people and Church because you call us each moment to be so. Give us your Spirit so we can keep saying "yes" to you and Jesus for the salvation of all peoples.

Resource

Catechism, 781-808

Glossary

Ministerial Priesthood. By Holy Orders, bishops, priests, and deacons are called to minister to the sanctification, guidance, and instruction of the faithful.

People of God. An image of the Church emphasized in Vatican II. God calls the people into community with the Trinity and each other to listen to his Word, offer a sacrifice of praise, and covenant with him and each other.

Priesthood of the Faithful. By Baptism all believers are initiated into the priesthood of all the faithful to offer a sacrifice of praise, witness Christ, and help sanctify the world.

Life Application

1. In what ways do I help my local parish become a faith community? What acts of service and charity do I offer to those in need in my parish? How do I support the growth of spiritual life there?
2. As a member of the priesthood of all the faithful, what am I doing for the sanctification of the world? What connection do I make between my faith and the workplace? What strategies do I use to share my faith with others?
3. What have I done to foster vocations to the priesthood and religious life? How can I help priests and religious live up to their calling? How can priests and religious help me to fulfill my calling either to married life or the single life?

Focus

. . . Look for a moment at the whole great panorama of twenty centuries [of the Church]. It begins in the wounded side of Christ on Calvary, goes through the "tempering" of Pentecostal fires and comes onward like a burning flood to pass through each [era]. . . . Fresh living water springs up in us and new flames are lit. By virtue of the divine power received from her Founder the Church is an institution which endures; but even more than an institution, she is a life that is passed on. She sets the seal of unity on all the children of God whom she gathers together.

Henri De Lubac, S.J., *The Splendor of the Church*

Chapter 23

The Four Marks of the Church

"This is the sole Church of Christ, which in the Creed we profess to be one, holy, catholic and apostolic" (*Lumen Gentium*, 8).

Catechism, 811

St. Joan of Arc could see the holiness of the Church beyond the folly that confronted her. This nineteen-year-old woman faced an inquisitor's threatening question, "Do you consider yourself in the state of grace?" Boldly, she replied, "If I am, may God keep me there. If I am not, may God put me there."

The bishops reminded her they stood for the authority of the Church. Astutely, she shot back, "To me, the Church is where Christ is. There can be no contradiction between Christ and the Church."

Joan's faith perceived the signs of the Church even when its members failed to witness them. What are these signs and what do they mean? These signs are both realizations and challenges. They exist as true evidence of the Church's reality and presence, but while the Church is on pilgrimage there are challenges to live up to what the signs ask us to be.

1. *The Church is one.* The internal unity of the Church derives from the unity of God, the unifying work of Jesus and the Spirit. The bonds of unity are expressed in the confession of one faith, the communal celebration of divine worship, and the harmony of the membership. Jesus set Peter over the other apostles. In him Jesus established the visible and perpetual principle of unity. The Pope, as the successor of Peter, is the principle of unity for the bishops and the faithful. Bishops are the signs of unity in their dioceses.

This unity underlies diversity of particular Churches, within the Catholic communion, and a wide variety of cultural expressions. Historically, communities withdrew from Catholic communion. The ecumenical movement is a ministry directed to the restoration of the unity of all Christians.

2. *The Church is holy.* The holiness of the Church flows from an essential unity with Father, Son, and Spirit. Through the Church, Christ's saving holiness extends to its members and the world. The members of the Church must yet acquire this holiness. Holy Church, with sinners as members, must pursue constant penance and renewal. The canonization of saints, in whom the Spirit of holiness succeeded, is evidence of the holiness of the Church. The saints serve as models and intercessors. "[In Mary], the Church is already 'the all-holy' " (*Catechism*, 829).

3. *The Church is catholic.* The word *catholic* means "universal." The Church is catholic because Christ is present in it as Head to the Body. Jesus gives to the Church the fullness of the means of salvation, a confession of faith and full sacramental life. The Church is catholic because Jesus sends it to every member of the human race. Catholicity is a gift that cannot be lost and a task to be undertaken, especially that of mission and ecumenism.

4. *The Church is apostolic.* The Church is apostolic because it is founded on the apostles and sent on mission by the Risen Christ. The flow of leadership goes from Jesus to apostles to Pope and bishops. Jesus appointed Peter the head of the apostles. The Pope is his successor. The bishops are successors of the apostles. Pope and bishops form the "Magisterium" — the official teaching office of the Church, willed by Christ to assure the authentic transmission and interpretation of his teachings.

Reflection

1. **What is the "oneness" of the Church?**
   The Church is one in its divine trinitarian source. Pope and bishops are signs of unity. Ecumenism is meant to restore unity of divided Christians (cf. *Catechism*, 813-816).

2. **How is the Church holy?**
   Father, Son, and Spirit constitute the holiness of the Church. Sinners, through penance and renewal, strive for holiness. Mary and the saints exemplify the Church's holiness (cf. *Catechism*, 823-829).

3. **Why is the Church catholic?**
   "[The Church] proclaims the fullness of the faith. She bears in herself and administers the totality of the means of salvation. She is sent out to all peoples . . ." (*Catechism*, 868).

4. **What is apostolic about the Church?**
   "[The Church] is built on a lasting foundation: 'the twelve apostles of the Lamb' (Rev 21:14). She is upheld infallibly in the truth: Christ governs her through Peter and the other apostles, who are present in their successors, the Pope and the college of bishops" (*Catechism*, 869).

Prayer

I believe in one, holy, catholic, and apostolic Church. Lord help me to be a unifier, holy, catholic, and apostolic.

Resource

Catechism, 813-870

Glossary

Canonization. The Church process that examines the lives of members who exhibited heroic virtue and concludes they are now saints in heaven. They serve as models of Christian living and intercede for us.

Ecumenism. The movement to heed the call of Christ that all Christians should strive for unity.

Marks of the Church. Four signs that evidence the Church's presence in the world. She is one, holy, catholic, and apostolic. These marks are both realizations and challenges.

Life Application

1. What am I doing to overcome disunity in my family or among my friends where this situation exists? How do I help make my parish more of a community? When have I advanced the cause of ecumenism?
2. What do I think of when I am asked to be holy? What practices help me to be holy? How does liturgy initiate me into holiness? How are places and things made holy? How is my home a holy place?
3. Do I accept all the teachings of the Church? If I do not, how can I come to full faith? How would I help a "pick and choose" Catholic to come to full faith in all the Church's teachings?

Focus

. . . to be holy is not to be perfect yet. The Church's obvious human imperfections have been an occasion for scandal and apostasy for . . . centuries. But paradoxically this very fact is also a powerful argument for her divine nature. This is cleverly brought out in Boccaccio's story of Abraham, the medieval Jewish merchant in *The Decameron*. Abraham is contemplating becoming a Catholic. He tells his friend, the bishop of Paris, who has been trying unsuccessfully to convert him, that he has to go to Rome on business. The bishop is horrified: "Don't go! When you see the stupidity and corruption there, you'll never join the Church." (This was the time of the Medici Popes, who were notoriously worldly and corrupt.) But Abraham is a practical man. Business calls. Upon his return to France, he tells the bishop he is now ready to be baptized. The bishop is astounded, but Abraham explains: "I'm a practical businessman. No earthly business that stupid and corrupt could last fourteen weeks. Your Church has lasted fourteen centuries. It must have God behind it."

Peter Kreeft, *Fundamentals of the Faith*

Chapter 24

We Believe in the Communion of Saints

Sancta sanctis! ("God's holy gifts for God's holy people") is proclaimed by the celebrant in most Eastern liturgies during the elevation of the holy Gifts before the distribution of communion.

Catechism, 948

St. Anthony of Padua joined the Franciscans at age twenty-six. Short and plump, Anthony looked the merry friar. Indeed he cheered the faith of millions with his gift of preaching. Ranked among the doctors of the Church he is better known for finding our lost keys and missing wallets.

In the nineteenth century, a bakery owner named Louise Bouffier promised Anthony she would donate bread to the poor if he would help her locksmith open the intransigent lock on the door to her bakery. The saint obliged and the apostolate of St. Anthony's Bread began, a "food for the poor" program that endures to this day. Anthony continues to find things for us and inspire us to charitable giving.

Anthony's story illustrates the Church's teaching on the Communion of Saints. The teaching has several meanings. First it refers to the gifts and graces communicated to the members of the Church by Jesus, the head of the Church. Second, it speaks of the gifts the members share with each other.

Faith sharing is part of the picture. So also is participation in the sacraments, events of holiness that unite us to Christ. The charisms that come to our members from the Holy Spirit are another element in this vision. Acts of charitable giving, social concern, and every act of love illustrate the practical outcome of the Communion of Saints.

This teaching also points to the three states of the Church: those of us who are pilgrims on earth, those being purified in purgatory, and those who are in heaven. We are all united by Christ in one holy community.

This is the basis for the intercession of the saints. The dying St. Dominic said, "Do not weep. I shall be of more use to you in heaven than in my lifetime." St. Thérèse of the Child Jesus warmed us with her words, "I shall spend my heaven doing good upon earth."

Here on earth we ask each other to pray to God for our intentions. It is even more powerful to ask Mary and the saints in heaven who live with God in permanent love to pray for us.

We believe our prayers for our brothers and sisters in purgatory are effective. "[F]rom the earliest days of the Christian religion, [the Church] has honored with great respect the memory of the dead . . . 'because it is a holy and wholesome thought to pray for the dead, that they may be loosed from their sins' (2 Mac 12:46)" (*Dogmatic Constitution on the Church*, 50; SVC).

In a special way, the liturgies of All Saints and All Souls are celebrations of the Communion of Saints. Taken together they form a masterpiece of prayer and a vision of the community of all the redeemed in heaven, purgatory, and on earth.

On earth the saints are pilgrims in the process of formation. In purgatory, the saints are in the final stage of purification. In heaven the saints are fixed in glory by the grace of Christ. Prayer and love unite us all in Jesus Christ.

Reflection

1. *What spiritual gifts are shared in the Communion of Saints?*
    On earth the members of the Church share faith with one another, share in the graces of the sacraments, benefit from one another's charisms, practice love for one another, charitable giving, and social concern (cf. *Catechism*, 949-953).

2. *What are the three states of the Church?*
    ". . . some of [Christ's] disciples are pilgrims on earth. Others have died and are being purified, while still others are in glory, contemplating 'in full light, God himself triune and one, exactly as he is' (*Lumen Gentium*, 49)" (*Catechism*, 954).

3. *What do we believe about interceding with God for one another?*
    On earth we pray to God for one another's intentions. We also pray for those in purgatory. We ask Mary and the saints in heaven to pray for us. We believe these prayers are effective because of Christ's love and mercy (cf. *Catechism*, 957-958).

Prayer

O Jesus, you are head of the body of all the saints, pilgrims on earth, those being purified in purgatory, and the blessed in heaven. You are our one mediator with the Father. May our prayers for each other touch your loving heart.

Resource

Catechism, 946-962

Glossary

Communion of Saints. The spiritual community of those of us who are still pilgrims on earth, then our brothers and sisters in the stage of purification in purgatory, and those who enjoy eternal glory and love of the Trinity in heaven along with the angels.

Intercessory Prayer. The prayer we offer for one another on earth and for those in purgatory. The prayer we ask from Mary and the saints on our behalf before the throne of God.

Life Application

1. Who are my favorite saints? What do I know about my patron saint? Which virtues of saints do I try to imitate? When do I find myself asking saints for help? Do I have a book of saints' lives at home? Which lives of the saints have I read?

2. How often do I pray for the souls in purgatory? When do I remember to pray for my departed parents, relatives, and friends? What does All Saints' Day and All Souls' Day mean to me?

3. How conscious am I of the angels and my guardian angel? When are the feasts of the angels Raphael, Gabriel, and Michael, and guardian angels? How might I pray for the intercession of angels on behalf of my family and friends?

Focus

It is therefore quite clear that all Christians in any state or walk of life are called to the fullness of Christian life and to the perfection of love, and by this holiness a more human manner of life is fostered also in earthly society. In order to reach this perfection the faithful should use their strength dealt out to them by Christ's gift, so that, following in his footsteps and conforming to his image, doing the will of God in everything, they may wholeheartedly devote themselves to the glory of God and to the service of their neighbor.

Dogmatic Constitution on the Church, 40; SVC

It is one thing to live with the saints in glory. To live with them on earth is another story.

Anonymous

Chapter 25

Mary Is the Mother of the Church

"[Mary] is 'clearly the mother of the members of Christ' . . . since she has by her charity joined in bringing about the birth of believers in the Church, who are members of its head" (*Lumen Gentium*, 53).

Catechism, 963

A young Catholic boy was telling a university professor who lived next door about the greatness of our Blessed Mother. The professor made fun of the boy by saying, "There is no difference between her and my mother." Just as nimbly, the boy replied, "That's what you think. But there is a heck of a lot of difference between the sons."

And yet there is also a special difference between the mothers too. Mary is no ordinary woman. Mary is the Mother of God. She is also the Mother of the Church. On the Cross, Jesus said to John, "Behold, your mother." Then to Mary, "Woman, behold, your son" (Jn 19:26-27).

In calling her mother, Jesus referred to her biological parentage. In naming her woman, he spoke of her theological parentage of the Church.

As a dutiful son, Jesus made sure someone would take care of his mother after he was gone. As the founder of the Church, Jesus commissioned Mary to share in the Church's birth by serving as the chief model of faith and love discipleship. Mary also is the woman whose powerful contemplation would affect the growth of the Church because of her union with Christ.

"[All] the Blessed Virgin's salutary influence on men . . . flows forth from the superabundance of the merits of Christ, rests on his mediation, depends entirely on it and draws all its power from it" (*Lumen Gentium*, 60; SVC).

After the ascension of Jesus, Mary joined the community of believers in the Upper Room and prayed for the gift of the Spirit. Just as she was maternally present at the Incarnation of Jesus at Bethlehem, so she is maternally present at the birth of the Mystical Body of Christ at Pentecost.

Finally, the Immaculate Virgin, kept free of original sin, completed the course of her life on earth and was raised, body and soul, to the glory of heaven. "In your childbearing you remain a virgin. In your dormition [assumption] you have not left the world, O Mother of God. You have rejoined the source of life. You, who conceived the living God and who, by your prayers, will deliver our souls from death" (Byzantine Troparion for the feast of the Dormition, August 15).

The Church honors Mary with a special veneration. From the earliest days of Christianity, the faithful have honored Mary as Mother of God and prayed for her protection from dangers and her help for their needs. This veneration of Mary is essentially different from the adoration given to Father, Son, and Spirit. It finds its expression in the liturgical feasts dedicated to the Mother of God.

Finally, Mary is a sign of hope about our eternal future. "She is the image of the Church's attainment of glory in the age that is to come. Here on earth, until the day of the Lord comes, she is the resplendent sign of sure hope and a comfort to the People of God on their pilgrimage" (*Lumen Gentium*, 68; SVC).

Reflection

1. *Is Mary just our model of faith discipleship?*

   "By her complete adherence to the Father's will, to his Son's redemptive work, and to every prompting of the Holy Spirit, the Virgin Mary is the Church's model of faith and charity. . . .

   "Her role in relation to the Church and to all humanity goes still further. 'In a wholly singular way she cooperated by her obedience, faith, hope, and burning charity in the Savior's work of restoring supernatural life to souls. For this reason she is a mother to us in the order of grace' (*Lumen Gentium*, 61)" (*Catechism*, 967-968).

2. *What is the Church's teaching about Mary's assumption?*

   "The Most Blessed Virgin Mary, when the course of her earthly life was completed, was taken up body and soul into the glory of heaven, where she already shares in the glory of her Son's Resurrection, anticipating the resurrection of all members of his Body" (*Catechism*, 974).

3. *Should we honor Mary and pray for her intercession?*

   We venerate Mary for her faith and obedience. We pray for her intercession as our heavenly Mother (cf. *Catechism*, 971).

Prayer

Remember, O most gracious Virgin Mary, that never was it known that anyone who fled to your protection, implored your help, or sought your intercession, was left unaided. Inspired by this confidence, I fly unto you, O Virgin of virgins, my Mother. To you I come, before you I stand, sinful and sorrowful. O Mother of the Word Incarnate, despise not my petitions, but in your mercy hear and answer me. Amen.

Resource

Catechism, 963-975

Glossary

Assumption. The doctrine that Mary was raised, body and soul, into the glory of heaven.

Mother of the Church. At Calvary Jesus entrusted his mother to John. Then he said, "Woman, behold, your son." Jesus made Mary our spiritual mother and Mother of the Church. This became more evident at Pentecost. Just as Mary was the physical mother of Jesus at Bethlehem, she became the spiritual mother of the Mystical Body of Christ at Pentecost.

Life Application

1. Mary is the model for my faith life. What can I learn about my faith development from these scenes from Mary's life: Annunciation? Her visit to Elizabeth? The birth scene at Bethlehem? Simeon telling her a sword will pierce her heart? The miracle at Cana? The foot of the Cross? Pentecost?
2. Mary is also my spiritual mother as well as Mother of the Church. What ways do I show devotion to Mary? What practices would enrich my Marian devotion? How clearly do I connect my relation to Mary with her essential link to Christ?
3. How often do I say the Rosary? Do I encourage members of my family to say the Rosary? How can I promote Rosary devotion? Have I made pilgrimages to Marian shrines? Which ones? How did it help my faith growth?

Focus

It is not really surprising that the Church knows this truth concerning Mary's holy ending. . . . For if the content of Mary's life is known, something can be said about the outcome and fruit of that life. The Church knows Mary's true identity, how she lived, what her importance in the divine plan of redemption was, and the part she played in the one great drama of sacred history. The Church knows how far advanced this one history of mankind is already, into the Last Days, in fact that have come upon us since the Resurrection of our Lord. . . . For that reason the Church can . . . say that Mary, with the whole reality of her life — with body and soul, therefore — has entered into that perfect fulfillment which every Christian hopes for from the grace of God, as the one outcome and fruit of his own human life.

Karl Rahner, S.J., *Mary, Mother of God*

Chapter 26

The Forgiveness of Our Sins

> The Apostles' Creed associates faith in the forgiveness of sins not only with faith in the Holy Spirit, but also with faith in the Church and in the communion of saints.
>
> *Catechism,* 976

A priest was hearing children's confessions. A little boy came in and confessed, "I threw peanuts in the river." The amused priest absolved the boy and sent him on his way. The second penitent came in and also said, "I threw peanuts in the river." Tolerantly, the priest forgave him and dismissed him. A third little boy came in. Before the child could say anything, the priest said, "I suppose you threw peanuts in the river." "No, Father," said the boy. "I am Peanuts."

Whether the issue is lighthearted or serious, we all need God's forgiveness. We are meant to be God's friends. But original and actual sin get in the way. Our faith calls us to believe that God always approaches us with forgiveness, so that sin will not break our friendship with him. Reconciliation with God not only makes us God's friends, but also heals our relations with all other people.

In the second part of this *Catechism,* we will treat more explicitly the forgiveness of sins in the sacraments of Baptism and Reconciliation.

Jesus connected the forgiveness of sins to faith and Baptism. Just before his ascension, the risen Jesus commissioned his apostles to evangelize the world. "Go into the whole world and proclaim the gospel to every creature. Whoever believes and is baptized will be saved" (Mk 16:15). In our first profession of faith and our Baptism, God purifies us from all sin, original and actual.

But the four wounds of original sin remain: (1) a mind that finds it hard to know truth; (2) a will that is weak in choosing good; (3) a heart that can tend to malice; (4) emotions and passions that are disordered. Nature's weaknesses stay with us. We sin again. God's loving mercy also abides with us. Jesus gave us the Sacrament of Reconciliation to provide us with the forgiveness which restores our friendship with God and the ecclesial community.

The Church joyfully engages in this ministry of reconciliation received from God. "[A]ll this is from God, who has reconciled us to himself through Christ and has given us the ministry of reconciliation" (2 Cor 5:18).

John's gospel tells us that on Easter night, Jesus appeared to the apostles. His first word was "Peace," a message of reconciliation. His first act was to breathe on them, giving them the Spirit who would make "peace" happen. He followed this with a commission to forgive sins. "Whose sins you forgive are forgiven" (Jn 20:23).

God the Father had breathed into Adam the breath of life. Now God the Son breathed into the apostles, the Holy Spirit, the breath of divine life, and the power to forgive sins. They, in turn, passed this power onto others through ordination.

The forgiveness of our sins is a grace. Risen, Jesus convinces us death can be overcome. Commissioning the apostles, Jesus assures us our sins are forgivable. Jesus wore the nail marks of the Passion that night, signs of our salvation from sin. No source of joy could be greater for our personal lives.

Reflection

1. *What is the creed's context for the forgiveness of sins?*
   "The Creed links 'the forgiveness of sins' with its profession of faith in the Holy Spirit, for the risen Christ entrusted to the apostles the power to forgive sins when he gave them the Holy Spirit" (*Catechism*, 984).

2. *Who gives the Church the power to forgive sins?*
   "By Christ's will, the Church possesses the power to forgive the sins of the baptized and exercises it through bishops and priests normally in the sacrament of Penance" (*Catechism*, 986).

3. *What is the priests' and sacraments' role in forgiving sins?*
   "In the forgiveness of sins, both priests and sacraments are instruments which our Lord Jesus Christ, the only author and liberal giver of salvation, wills to use in order to efface our sins and give us the grace of justification" (*Catechism*, 987).

Prayer

O Lord, be merciful to me, a sinner. Reconcile me to yourself and to the Church. Enable me to forgive others as generously as you have forgiven me.

Resource

Catechism, 976-987

Glossary

Forgiveness of Sins. The purpose of Christ's redeeming work is to free us from our sins and free us for the divine life which we will enjoy fully in heaven.

Reconciliation. A way of describing what happens when our sins are forgiven in the sacraments of Baptism and Penance, wherein we are reconciled to God, others, and self.

Life Application

1. Am I aware of my sinfulness and therefore the need for God's forgiveness? How did I arrive at that awareness? What does my experience tell me about sin? When I receive absolution in the Sacrament of Reconciliation, do I feel reunited to God, Church, and myself? I know that God forgives me. Do I forgive myself?

2. When others offend me, which of the following options do I take: (a) that they must apologize before I forgive them; (b) that I forgive them so they can apologize; or (c) that I will never forgive them? Explain your choice.

3. What lessons about forgiveness can I draw from these biblical stories: Christ's forgiveness of the woman taken in adultery; Christ's forgiveness of the Good Thief on the cross; Christ's forgiveness of the sins of the paralytic even before he cures him?

Focus

On a Christmas Eve during the Vietnam War, the commander of the Hoa Loa prison camp distributed Bibles to the American prisoners. He told them they could keep the Bibles just for Christmas Day.

The American soldiers decided to make the best use of this chance. They would make copies of Bible texts. They used toilet paper for writing pads, fence wire for pens. They made ink out of toothpaste and ashes.

And these American prisoners who had every reason to be angry and unforgiving with their Vietnamese captors copied down first of all the parable of the Forgiving Father and the Prodigal Son.

Chapter 27

The Resurrection of Our Bodies

Belief in the resurrection of the dead has been an essential element of the Christian faith from its beginnings.

Catechism, 991

Ancient Egyptians embalmed their pharaohs' bodies so well that the dried remains exist to this day. Some moderns resort to cryonics, freezing their dead bodies in the hope of coming back in the future. The yearning to save the body from the ravages of death is as old as human nature. The trouble is that the bodies are still dead, whether they rest in a fifty-story pyramid in Cairo or a freezer in Los Angeles.

Most cultures and religions have despaired of saving the bodies and concentrate on the durability of the souls. But our Church is different. We definitely believe in the immortality of the soul. But we also affirm the resurrection of the body. Catholicism is interested in the sanctity of the deceased body and retains the bodies of saints for relics. But the real bodily focus of our faith is on the transformation of our old dead bodies into the new bodies resurrected in Christ on the Last Day.

The Gospels tell us the Pharisees believed in the resurrection, but the Sadducees did not. Jesus clearly taught resurrection and rebuked the Sadducees for not believing in it. "Are you not misled because you do not know the scriptures or the power of God" (Mk 12:24). Jesus declared that he himself was the source of resurrection. "I am the resurrection and the life" (Jn 11:25).

Just as he raised Lazarus and others from the dead, so he will raise us too. "[E]veryone who sees the Son and believes in him may have eternal life, and I shall raise him [on] the last day" (Jn 6:40).

The Catholic Church teaches that after death, the soul lives on and goes to meet God for judgment. The body decays. The soul awaits the end of time when God will restore it to the resurrected body which will share either eternal life in heaven or punishment in hell.

All people will rise from the dead. They will have the same bodies they had in life, but changed. St. Paul uses seed-plant imagery to explain this. "With what kind of body will the dead be brought back? . . . What you sow is not the body that is to be, but a bare kernel of wheat. God gives it a body as he chooses. . . So it is with the resurrection of the dead. It is sown corruptible. It is raised incorruptible. It is sown a natural body. It is raised a spiritual body" (cf. 1 Cor 15:35-37; 42-44). When will this happen? On the Last Day, at the end of the world.

Because of our Baptism and life of grace in the sacraments, especially in the Eucharist, we are already sharing in the risen life of Jesus. We have died to sin and risen to divine life in Jesus. We possess even now the kind of life we will have in heaven. Because our whole being shares in grace, even our bodies, temples of the Spirit, have an advanced experience of eternal life, though our bodies will die and only know transformation at the end of time.

Our Eucharistic life demonstrates this. Jesus says, "Whoever eats my flesh and drinks my blood has eternal life [right now] and I will raise him on the last day" (Jn 6:54). Yes, Lord, we believe you are our life today, tomorrow, and forever.

Reflection

1. *Why is there death?*

   "In a sense bodily death is natural, but for faith it is in fact the 'wages of sin' (Rom 6:23)."

   "The Church's Magisterium, as authentic interpreter of the affirmations of Scripture and Tradition, teaches that death entered the world on account of man's sin" (*Catechism*, 1006, 1008).

2. *What happens after death?*

   "In death, the separation of the soul from the body, the human body decays and the soul goes to meet God, while awaiting its reunion with its glorified body" (*Catechism*, 997).

3. *Will our risen bodies be the same as our earthly ones?*

   " 'We believe in the true resurrection of this flesh that we now possess' (Council of Lyons II: DS 854). We sow a corruptible body in the tomb, but he raises up an incorruptible body, a 'spiritual body' (cf. 1 Cor 15:42-44)" (*Catechism*, 1017).

Prayer

Jesus, I hear and believe the words of Scripture: "I will raise you up. I will raise you up on the last day" (Jn 6:40).

Resource

Catechism, 976-1019

Glossary

Immortality. Means the soul lives on after death. Our faith teaches us the soul will be reunited to our resurrected bodies at the Second Coming of Jesus.

Resurrected Body. By the power of God our earthly bodies will rise again, transformed by the Spirit at the resurrection of the dead. Read 1 Corinthians 15.

Wages of Sin. Phrase from Romans 6:23 which says that faith tells us that the moral reason for death is sin.

Life Application

1. What are three experiences I have had which strengthen my belief in the immortality of my soul? Were there times in my life when I doubted this? If so, why? How would I teach young people, so full of life, that death is real and souls are immortal?
2. Why does the Church insist on the sanctity of the body? What Church rituals and ceremonies reinforce this belief? How does the seed-plant image help me to envision what my spiritual, transformed body will be like at the resurrection?
3. If I were trying to persuade an unbeliever about the immortality of the soul, what approach would I take? Similarly, how would I present a convincing case for the resurrection of the body?

Focus

And death shall have no dominion,
Dead men naked they shall be one
With the man in the wind and the west moon;
When their bones are picked clean
and the clean bones gone,
They shall have stars at elbow and foot;
Though they go mad they shall be sane,
Though they sink through the sea
they shall rise again;
Though lovers be lost, lost shall not;
And death shall have no dominion.

Dylan Thomas, "And Death Shall Have No Dominion"

Chapter 28

What Happens After Death?

The Christian who unites his own death to that of Jesus views it as a step towards him and an entrance into everlasting life.

Catechism, 1020

Some scientists report several thousand cases of "life after death" experiences. People who were declared clinically dead tell us of their experiences of the beyond. "I viewed my body from the back. I still felt as though I had an entire body, while I was outside my body. I felt like a feather . . . I could see light. It grew larger as I drew near it. I felt that it was Christ."

Such statements do not scientifically prove we are immortal, but they reinforce what Christian faith has affirmed for two thousand years. Is there life after death? Yes!

When the Church has absolved dying persons from sins, sealed them with anointing, and given them Jesus in Viaticum (last Eucharist), she speaks with sweet assurance: "Go forth, Christian soul! . . . May holy Mary, the angels, and all the saints come to meet you as you go forth from this life. . . . May you see your Redeemer face to face." The soul faces a "particular judgment." Each one of us goes immediately either to heaven or to hell or to purgatory. Death and this judgment and the three outcomes are often called the "four last things." Here are the three outcomes:

1. *Heaven.* Those who die in friendship and grace with God, and who are perfectly purified, will live forever with Christ. They will see God face to face as he really is. This perfect life with the Holy Trinity, with the Virgin Mary, the angels, and the saints is called heaven. Heaven is the ultimate goal and realization of the deepest human desires. It is a state of supreme and definitive happiness.

2. *Purgatory.* Those who die in the grace and friendship of God, but who are not fully purified from sinfulness, are assured of their eternal salvation. But they must still undergo a purification to obtain the holiness needed to enter heaven. This is purgatory. In the liturgy of All Souls, the Church remembers this teaching and recommends Eucharist, prayer, charitable giving, and works of penance on behalf of the departed.

3. *Hell.* We cannot be united to God unless we freely choose to love him. We do not love God if we sin gravely against him, our neighbor, or ourselves. To die in mortal sin without repentance and recourse to God's mercy means we have separated ourselves from him by a deliberate and

free choice. This definitive self-exclusion from communion with God is called hell.

Scripture and the teaching of the Church on heaven and hell emphasize a call to personal responsibility by which we use our freedom, aided by divine grace, to affect our eternal destiny. There is always an urgent call to conversion and repentance. God predestines no one to hell. Only a free turning away from God in mortal sin and persistence in this attitude leads to hell. The Church prays every day in her liturgy for conversion of her members (2 Pt 3:9).

While we use earthly images, both physical and psychological, to describe heaven, hell, and purgatory, none of them comprehensively describes these realities. It is better to concentrate on sinless, loving choices, moral and spiritual responsibility, and lifelong conversion to Jesus Christ.

Reflection

1. *What is the "particular judgment"?*

   "Each man receives his eternal retribution in his immortal soul at the very moment of his death, in a particular judgment that refers his life to Christ: either entrance into the blessedness of heaven — through a purification or immediately — or immediate and everlasting damnation" (*Catechism*, 1022).

2. *What should we learn from the Church's doctrine about hell?*

   "The affirmations of Sacred Scripture and the teachings of the Church on the subject of hell are a call to the responsibility incumbent upon man to make use of his freedom in view of his eternal destiny. They are at the same time an urgent call to conversion: 'Enter by the narrow gate; for the gate is wide and the way is easy, that leads to destruction . . .' (Mt 7:13)" (*Catechism*, 1036).

3. *Why are images poor descriptions of realities after death?*

   "This mystery of blessed communion with God and all who are in Christ is beyond all understanding and description. Scripture speaks of it in images: life, light, peace, . . . 'no eye has seen, nor ear heard . . . what God has prepared for those who love him' (1 Cor 2:9)" (*Catechism*, 1027).

Prayer

Merciful Judge, fill me with the grace of responsibility that I may make choices which lead me to heaven and eternal life.

Resource

Catechism, 1020-1037

Glossary

Four Last Things. These are death/particular judgment, heaven, hell, and purgatory.

Heaven. A state of supreme happiness for those who die in grace and friendship with God, and whose souls are purified from all sin. This life of perfect happiness with the Holy Trinity, the angels, and saints is called heaven.

Hell. Those who die in mortal sin have separated themselves from God by a free choice. This definitive self-exclusion from communion with God is called hell.

Particular Judgment. Immediately after death we are judged by God as to whether we go to purgatory, heaven, or hell.

Purgatory. Those who die in the friendship of God, but are not yet purified from sinfulness, undergo a purification in purgatory to prepare them for heaven.

Life Application

1. Surveys say that most Americans believe in God, heaven, and hell. And most Americans think they are going to heaven. What do I think? Are we too optimistic about our chances for heaven? What is a more realistic approach?

2. Purgatory is a teaching of the Church. How does the feast of All Souls support this teaching? What prayers do I say for my departed relatives and friends? Why do some people have difficulty with the doctrine of purgatory? How can I help them accept it?

3. How do canonization ceremonies and the feasts of the saints reinforce the doctrine of the particular judgment? If I were to live each day as though it were my last, what difference would that make in my behavior? How can I be responsible for my eternal destiny?

Focus

Political and military leaders have always found ways to assure secular immortality. Pharaohs built pyramids. American presidents have libraries. The kings of England often are enshrined in English cathedrals in massive stone tombs. These secular efforts symbolize the hunger for real immortality.

The poet Shelley captures this in his poem about Ramses II from the thirteenth century B.C. who built a monument to himself. All that is left now are two trunkless legs of stone, leaving the frowned and wrinkled head lying in the sand. An inscription says:

My name is Ozymandias, king of kings:
Look on my works, ye mighty, and despair.
Nothing besides remains. Round the decay
Of that colossal wreck, boundless and bare
The lone and level sands stretch far away.

The poor man must have been terribly insecure to insist so much on his ability to scare people. It is a poor solution.

How different our churches with their altars of the death and Resurrection of Jesus Christ. These structures of faith are signs of hope, immortality, and our victory over death.

Chapter 29

The Last Judgment

> The resurrection of all the dead, "of both the just and the unjust," will precede the Last Judgment. . . . The Last Judgment will come when Christ returns in glory.
>
> *Catechism*, 1038, 1040

Michelangelo's mighty fresco of the Last Judgment covers the wall behind the altar in the Sistine Chapel. A legend claims that a cardinal disliked the artist's use of nudity and harassed him about it. Irritated, Michelangelo put him in the fresco, writhing in hell. Outraged, the cardinal said to the Pope, "Make him take me out of there." Amused, the Pope replied, "Eminence, you know very well I can only help people get out of purgatory."

Scripture states clearly that God will judge our behavior. "You render to everyone according to his deeds" (Ps 62:12). The New Testament repeated this often. Jesus said, "For the Son of Man will come with his angels in his Father's glory, and then he will repay everyone according to his conduct" (Mt 16:27). In the parable of the Last Judgment, the supreme judge divides the "sheep" from the "goats" according to their deeds of love. "[W]hatever you did for one of these least brothers of mine, you did for me" (Mt 25:40).

The New Testament vividly describes Christ's Second Coming (Mt 24; Mk 13; and the book of Revelation, especially chapter 21). Some have thought they could figure out the exact date of Christ's coming. They have always been wrong. Jesus taught us not to bother with this for we cannot know the "day and hour" (Mt 24:36). We should view the Second Coming of Jesus and the Last Judgment as signs of hope that God will finally establish the rule of love, justice, mercy, and salvation which overcomes all evil and death.

Those who have already experienced the particular judgment will not have a "second trial" at the general judgment. They will, however, be reunited to their resurrected and transfigured bodies which will share in their eternal destinies.

Will the world end at the Second Coming? The world as we know it, distorted by sin and evil, will cease to be. At the same time Scripture speaks of a "new heaven and a new earth" (cf. 2 Pt 3:10-13 and Rv 21:1). St. Paul says, "For creation awaits with eager expectation the revelation of the children of God; for creation was made subject to futility, not of its own accord but because of the one who subjected it, in hope that creation itself would be set free from slavery to corruption and share in the glorious freedom of the children of God" (Rom 8:19-21).

Vatican II teaches, "We know neither the moment of the consummation of the earth and of man, nor the way the universe will be transformed. The form of this world, distorted by sin, is passing away and we are taught that God is preparing a new dwelling and a new earth in which righteousness dwells, whose happiness will fill and surpass all the desires of peace in the hearts of men" (*Gaudium et Spes*, 39; SVC).

George Frideric Handel concludes his stirring oratorio *Messiah* with the "Amen Chorus." Similarly, the *Catechism* finishes its explanation of the creed with an "Amen!" In Hebrew, *Amen* comes from the same root as the word "believe." The term connotes solidity, reliability, and fidelity. *Amen* speaks both of God's faithfulness to us and of our confidence in him. We started with, "I believe." We end with "Amen!" Yes, Lord, I believe in you and what you have taught me. I trust you. I love you. Help me to be and become what my faith implies.

Reflection

1. *What will happen at the Last Judgment?*
    "At the end of time, the Kingdom of God will come in its fullness. Then the just will reign with Christ for ever, glorified in body and soul, and the material universe itself will be transformed. God will then be 'all in all' (1 Cor 15:28), in eternal life" (*Catechism*, 1060).

2. *What should we be doing before the Second Coming?*
    " '. . . the expectancy of a new earth should spur us on. . . . That is why, although we must be careful to distinguish earthly progress clearly from the increase of the kingdom of Christ, such progress is of vital concern to the kingdom of God, insofar as it can contribute to the better ordering of human society' (*Gaudium et Spes*, 39)" (*Catechism*, 1049).

3. *Why is "Amen!" a fitting ending for the creed?*
    "In Hebrew, amen comes from the same root as the word 'believe.' "
    "[The] Creed's final 'Amen!' repeats and confirms its first words: 'I believe' " (*Catechism*, 1062, 1064).

Prayer

Thank you, Lord, for the gift of faith. Help then my unbelief and make my faith abound that I may seek where you are found.

Resource

Catechism, 1038-1065

Glossary

Last Judgment. Scripture teaches there will be a final judgment in which God makes visible for all to see the victory of Jesus over sin. The kingdom of God will arrive in its fullness, the world will be transfigured and the just will reign with Christ in glory.

Second Coming. Connected to the Last Judgment, Christ's Second Coming in glory will be associated with his separation of the saved from the damned. We do not know when this will happen.

Amen. From the Hebrew word for belief, it connotes fidelity and is a fitting conclusion to the beginning of the creed's words, "I believe."

Life Application

1. Why does modern secular culture seem so unwilling to accept a final divine judgment on how people choose to live their moral lives? What do I think of the judgments made by our local courts and the supreme court? If everyone I know feels free to make lots of judgments, why do they resist the idea that God will also feel free to judge us?

2. When God is denied the right to hold our feet to the fire and hold us accountable for our moral (or immoral) choices, what effect does this have on society? What are some persuasive arguments supporting our faith in a Last Judgment?

3. If there were no Second Coming of Jesus and no Last Judgment, what loss would there be for our religious and moral lives? Why is it important for us to realize we cannot know the hour or the day of the Second Coming?

Focus

Swedish filmmaker Ingmar Bergman, made a movie about the medieval "black death," titled *The Seventh Seal*. The theme is drawn from Revelation 8:1: "When he [the Lamb] broke open the seventh seal, there was silence in heaven for about half an hour."

A medieval knight returns to Scandinavia at the height of the plague. He beholds a land gripped with terror. People eat, drink, and play in desperation. He observes witch burnings and hears wild sermons about soul disease causing God's anger. Penitents roam the streets whipping themselves to appease God. Rape, looting, and pillaging prevail.

He meets a juggler's family — Joseph, Mary, and little Michael, whose name means "one who is like God." They do not share in the fanatic negativity of the age. They remain faith-filled, wondrous, and playful. They grieve over suffering and help where they can. It is the only light the knight sees, but it fails to convince him.

He believes the Lamb has opened the seventh seal, that heaven is silent; God is not listening or speaking. He returns to his castle where everyone despairingly waits, huddled for death. In the end the knight leads his family in the dance of death along the cliffs by the sea.

It is a film about lost faith in God's mercy, love, and powerful providence. It hears not the other side of the story of the judgment: "Come, you who are blessed by my Father. Inherit the kingdom prepared for you from the foundation of the world" (Mt 25:34).

Part Two

Sacraments: The Faith Celebrated

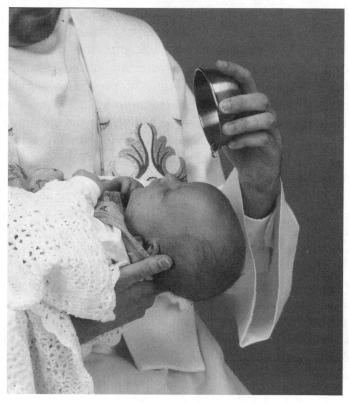

Chapter 30

Liturgy as Paschal Mystery

> . . . the Church celebrates in the liturgy above all the Paschal mystery
> by which Christ accomplished the work of our salvation.
>
> *Catechism*, 1067

An angel of fire branded the body of St. Francis of Assisi with the marks of
the five wounds of Jesus. An electric wire fatally burned the body of Trappist
monk Thomas Merton. Francis carried the cross of poverty. Merton bore the
cross of monastic solitude. They witnessed the Paschal mystery by dying to
self and living for God and others. Francis sought to heal us of greed. Merton
hoped to cure us of warlikeness and a taste for injustice.

Saints and outstanding Christian witnesses present hints of the richness
of Christ's Paschal mystery experienced in the liturgy. It is a mystery because
it is an action of God. It is paschal because it is a dying-rising experience.

Paschal mystery speaks of Christ's saving work in his death, Resurrec-
tion, ascension, and sending of the Spirit. It is always a dying-rising process.
The word *liturgy* comes from the Greek and means "people's work." The
Church has applied the word to the work of God's people at worship.

Historically, Jesus performed the work of salvation once and for all. Sacramentally, Jesus makes present his saving act in the Liturgy of Word and
Sacrament. This accomplishes the Father's divine plan of love for us. This
wondrous mystery becomes possible because of the presence and power of
the Holy Spirit at liturgical celebrations. Liturgy is a trinitarian event. Through
the Church and the sacraments this is available for us.

At liturgy God calls us to experience salvation. We respond in faith. We
need "ears to hear" in faith the saving words of the Word proclaimed to us.
We need "eyes to see" in faith the divine realities made visible in the rituals
and signs. We need "an understanding heart" in faith to surrender to the
covenant action taking place.

The book of Revelation and the letter to the Hebrews describe heavenly
liturgies. Revelation portrays Christ being sung to and adored for his gracious salvation. St. Paul's letter to the Hebrews pictures Jesus as the one true
High Priest offering forever his sacrifice for our redemption. Both books
shine with glory, joy, praise, songs, and rituals. Our earthly liturgies make
present this divine splendor and saving reality.

At the same time, the Church assembles us as God's people, led by bishop
and priest to offer sacrifice, praise, adoration, and thanksgiving to the Fa-

ther, through the Son, in the Spirit. We are made more profoundly an intimate community of faith by our contact with that heavenly community and through the graces and gifts received from the powerful action of the Holy Spirit at liturgy.

God calls us to live out the consequences of the Paschal mystery, celebrated at liturgy, by practicing and witnessing love, mercy, and justice in our families, neighborhoods, and society. We must die to our selfishness that we may rise to love of God, others, and self. Armed with the Word of God, nourished with the sacrament of God, and renewed by the Spirit, we go forth from liturgy as living Paschal mysteries. All is faith and all is grace. The benefits for humanity are abundant. Let us share our faith by word and deed. Then others will begin to know what the Paschal mystery has done for us.

Reflection

1. *Why do we speak of liturgy as "Paschal mystery"?*

   "[Jesus] accomplished this [redemption] principally by the Paschal mystery of his blessed Passion, Resurrection from the dead, and glorious Ascension, whereby 'dying he destroyed our death, rising he restored our life.' . . . For this reason, the Church celebrates in the liturgy above all the Paschal mystery by which Christ accomplished the work of our salvation" (*Catechism*, 1067).

2. *What is the relation between catechesis and liturgy?*

   "[Liturgy is] the privileged place for catechizing the People of God. 'Catechesis is intrinsically linked with the whole of liturgical and sacramental activity, for it is in the sacraments, especially in the Eucharist, that Christ Jesus works in fullness for the transformation of men' (Pope John Paul II, *Catechesi Tradendae*, 23)" (*Catechism*, 1074).

3. *What is the Holy Spirit's role in liturgy?*

   "The mission of the Holy Spirit in the liturgy of the Church is to prepare the assembly to encounter Christ; to recall and manifest Christ to the faith of the assembly; to make the saving work of Christ present and active by his transforming power; and to make the gift of communion bear fruit in the Church" (*Catechism*, 1112).

Prayer

Father, you call us to celebrate and live out the Paschal mystery of Jesus in the Church's liturgy by the Spirit's power. Help us to respond in faith by active participation in worship and Christian witness in our lives.

Resource
Catechism, 1066-1134

Glossary
Heavenly Liturgy. The letter to the Hebrews and the book of Revelation both describe the acts of worship in heaven by means of various images. Our earthly liturgy mirrors this heavenly one.

Liturgy. Comes from the Greek and means "people's work." The priesthood of all the faithful offer a sacrifice of praise. The ordained priest acts in the person of Christ to make Christ's saving action present.

Paschal Mystery. Liturgy is a mystery because of the divine action of Father, Son, and Spirit. It is Paschal because it makes present the dying-rising action of Jesus.

Life Application
1. I need "ears to hear" in faith the proclamation of the Word. How much do I study and pray the Bible so that I can do this more effectively at liturgy? In what way do I find the readings at liturgy deepening my faith?
2. I need "eyes to see" in faith the divine realities made visible in signs and rituals. How much does ritual awareness affect me at liturgy? What should I do to develop more in this area? What puzzles me about signs and rituals?
3. I need an "understanding heart" in faith to get in touch with the covenant action taking place. What proves to me that I am doing this? How would I share this faith experience with others?

Focus
Catechesis . . . cannot ignore the fact that [many people of our time] strongly sense a remoteness or even absence of God. This fact, which is part of the process of secularization, surely constitutes a danger for the faith; but it also impels us to have a purer faith and to become more humble in the presence of the mystery of God. With this perspective, it is possible to understand more easily the true nature of the worship which God demands and which glorifies him. . . . In the sacred liturgy, the faithful bring the fruits of every kind of act of charity, of justice, of peace, in order to make a humble offering of them to God, and to receive in return the words of life and the graces they need to . . . profess the truth in love . . . in communion with Christ, who offers his Body and Blood for [the salvation of the world.]
General Catechetical Directory, 48

Chapter 31

Why Call Liturgy a 'Celebration'?

Liturgy is an "action" of the whole Christ. . . .
Catechism, 1136

"Hell is other people!" So grumbles a character in a play by Sartre. Yet Sartre himself often went to celebrations like everyone else. People like to be with people. The Irish have a proverb that says, "It is better to quarrel than to be lonely."

Every culture in history has had forms of merry-making – drinking, feasting, and dancing. Why do people go to celebrations? (1) To get close to others. (2) To be happy. A celebration banishes workaday cares and releases us from the struggle for survival. (3) To feel solidarity. Celebrations give us a sense of belonging to a group that reinforces our identity and purpose.

Liturgies are celebrations in a similar sense. In celebrating the sacraments, we get close to heaven and one another in the Communion of Saints. Second, by faith we get in touch with the ultimate source of happiness which is the eternal life won for us by Jesus. Third, we strengthen our sense of solidarity with the whole Church. We feel we belong to the Body of Christ. This deepens our Catholic identity and sharpens our sense of purpose in this life.

The Church celebrates Christ's Paschal mystery with music, scriptural readings, homilies, processions, blessings, bread, wine, oil, arms outstretched in prayer, handshakes of peace, bowed heads, kneeling, standing, sitting, incense, holy water, flowers, candles, ritual vestments, choirs, organ, other instruments, and a distribution of roles and responsibilities for the priesthood of God's people and the ordained priesthood of bishop and priest and deacon.

The Church setting for the celebration uses many forms of architecture all the way from the simplicity of a modest chapel to the splendor of Gothic, Romanesque, Byzantine, Baroque, and contemporary styles. The worship space may have stained glass, sculpture, statues of Jesus, Mary, angels, and the saints. It may be made of marble, precious wood, gold, or silver. All are ways of praising God.

The worship space and the forms of worship communicate both the awesome transcendence of God and the intimacy of the community gathered to celebrate the gifts and graces of Jesus. Signs and symbols abound because of our need to get in touch with the divine presence. The Son of God honored us by becoming a man, the supreme icon of God. "He is the image of the invisible God" (Col 1:15). From the Incarnation onward, we have felt confident in using signs and symbols to help us experience the invisible presence of God.

Every parish church, chapel, and cathedral becomes for us a setting for celebrating the mysteries of salvation with a symphony of gestures, words, music, signs, and the glories of the worship space. Everything is coordinated for one purpose: to praise God for salvation and to enter into that mystery so we can experience again what Jesus has done for us. We are at once in the house of God, transported to the heavenly liturgy, and at the same time still on earth, journeying to the kingdom. Baptism equips us to do this. The Eucharist gives us bread for the journey. Such is the reason for calling liturgy a celebration. How richly God has blessed us!

Reflection

1. *Who are the celebrants at liturgy?*
   "It is the whole *community*, the Body of Christ united with its Head, that celebrates. 'Liturgical services are not private functions but are celebrations of the Church. . . . [Liturgical services] touch individual members of the Church in different ways, depending on their orders, their role in the liturgical services, and their actual participation in them' (*Sacrosanctum Concilium*, 26)" (*Catechism*, 1140).

2. *Why are signs and symbols used for the celebration?*
   "In human life, signs and symbols occupy an important place. As a being at once body and spirit, man expresses and perceives spiritual realities through physical signs and symbols. As a social being, man needs signs and symbols to communicate with others, through language, gestures, and actions. This same holds true for his relationship with God" (*Catechism*, 1146).

3. *What is the role of statues and icons?*
   "Christian iconography expresses in images the same Gospel message that Scripture communicates by words. Image and word illuminate each other. . . .

   "All the signs in the liturgical celebrations are related to Christ: as are sacred images of the holy Mother of God and of the saints as well" (*Catechism*, 1160-1161).

Prayer

"Exult, you just, in the Lord; / . . . Give thanks to the Lord on the harp; / with the ten-stringed lyre chant his praises."

Ps 33:1-2

Resource

Catechism, 1136-1162

Glossary

Immanence. Our experience of God as intimate with us in our earthly condition. This is especially true of our relation to Jesus in his humanity and to the Holy Trinity in sacramental celebrations. Immanence and transcendence describe two sides of one relationship.

Liturgy as Celebration. Refers to our joyful relation to the Holy Trinity, the angels and the full Communion of Saints. Secondly, it speaks to our union with the ultimate source of joy — the Trinity. Thirdly, it witnesses our solidarity with the whole Church on earth and the heavenly community beyond us.

Transcendence. Our experience of the divine, awesome presence of God as mystery and wholly other from us.

Life Application

1. If I go to a party, what do I expect? If I give a party, what do I want to happen? What would my life be like without any celebration? What elements of celebration do I like to see at liturgy?
2. Some liturgical celebrations concentrate so strongly on human fellowship that the divine aspect is missing. How would I correct that if asked? Why is it important to preserve the sense of mystery in liturgical celebration?
3. When have I felt most deeply moved by a liturgy? Why did I feel that way? Is it important that I always "get something" out of liturgy? What about "giving of myself?"

Focus

Just as many Americans are tone-deaf when it comes to symbols in language, so are they "body-deaf" when it comes to ritual. They simply do not get the point of it, at least when it is done in liturgy.

Yet American culture is not without its revered rituals. Think of the opening ceremonies at the Rose Bowl or Super Bowl. Perhaps the most awesome is the opening of the Olympics with the runner carrying the flame to light the great fire. Think of Mardi Gras and the Mummers Parade. Note the expected ritual surrounding the inauguration of the president, taps for the burial of military heroes, and the details associated with weddings: rice, streamers on the car, throwing the garter and the bride's bouquet, and the first dance of husband and wife.

Rituals do abound. The genius of Catholicism is its retention of basic ritual for worship while allowing for certain adaptations over time. Businessmen say, "Money talks." Worship says, "Ritual talks." Like a picture, a gesture is often worth a thousand words.

Chapter 32

Sacraments – The Body of Christ at Prayer

The Liturgy of the Hours . . . is like an extension of the Eucharistic celebration. . . .

Catechism, 1178

Rabbi Heschel once said that the essence of prayer is song. Sometimes the song is a joyful thanks for a grace received. Other times the song is sad – a lament for a loss. One man tells the story of being wild with grief over the loss of a daughter. He shared this one day with a stranger. She replied, "I never had a child." That healed the father and enabled him to thank God for the years he had with his daughter.

In the seven sacraments and the Liturgy of the Hours the Body of Christ is at prayer. It is the Church praying. St. Augustine asks us to identify with Jesus each time we engage in such prayer. "O Jesus, pray in us as the Head of the Body. Pray for us as our priest. We adore you as our God." The power of our prayer arises from the infinite persuasiveness of Jesus with whom we are united. The Father listens with love to his Son.

What are the sacraments of the Church? There are seven: Baptism, Confirmation (also called Chrismation), Eucharist, Reconciliation, Anointing of the Sick, Holy Orders, and Marriage. Jesus Christ instituted these sacraments. The sacraments are effective signs of grace. This means that each sacrament, by the power of the Spirit, creates in us the specific work of God intended by the sacrament.

Hence, Baptism, with its signs of water, oil, candle, and white vestment – plus the words and gestures – washes away all original and actual sin and initiates us into the Body of Christ. Of course, we must come with faith and the right disposition to receive these graces. Other sacramental celebrations happen in the same way. They illustrate the Body of Christ at prayer.

The Liturgy of the Hours prolongs the Eucharistic celebration. It contains psalms, hymns, canticles, readings from Scripture, the Fathers, writings of saints and doctors, texts of councils, responsories, and intercessory prayers. Sections are assigned for seven times each day. This is the Church at prayer, praising God constantly. It does not exclude popular devotion such as the Rosary, the Stations of the Cross, or worship of the Blessed Sacrament.

The praying Church also sets out for us the liturgical year. At the heart of this year is the Holy Triduum (Holy Thursday, Good Friday, Easter Vigil).

On a weekly basis Sunday is the regular focus of our worship. There is the time of the Manifestation of Jesus — Advent, Christmas, Epiphany. Then, the forty days of Lent preparing for the Triduum. Following this is the time between Easter and Pentecost when we contemplate the mysteries of salvation. After Pentecost we meditate on the Holy Spirit's work of conforming us to Christ.

Lastly, there are the feasts of the Blessed Mother and the saints. The Church honors Mary, the greatest outcome of the redemption. The Church remembers martyrs and other saints who exemplify the Paschal mystery. Such is the panorama of the Body of Christ at prayer. We are expected to have our private prayers and meditations. But we are called also to join in the powerful and effective prayer of the Church.

Reflection

1. *What are sacraments?*

   "The sacraments are efficacious signs of grace, instituted by Christ and entrusted to the Church, by which divine life is dispensed to us. The visible rites by which the sacraments are celebrated signify and make present the graces proper to each sacrament. They bear fruit in those who receive them with the required dispositions" (*Catechism*, 1131).

2. *What is the value of the Liturgy of the Hours?*

   "The faithful who celebrate the Liturgy of the Hours . . . [are] joined with [Christ's] unceasing and universal prayer that gives glory to the Father and implores the gift of the Holy Spirit on the whole world" (*Catechism*, 1196).

3. *What is the purpose of the liturgical year?*

   "In the liturgical year the various aspects of the one Paschal mystery unfold. . . .

   " 'In celebrating this annual cycle of the mysteries of Christ, Holy Church honors the Blessed Mary, Mother of God, with a special love. . . .'

   "When the Church keeps the memorials of martyrs and other saints during the annual cycle, she proclaims the Paschal mystery in those 'who have suffered and have been glorified. . . . She proposes them to the faithful as examples . . .' (*Sacrosanctum Concilium*, 103, 104)" (*Catechism*, 1171-1173).

Prayer

Lord Jesus, pray in us as Head of the Body. Pray for us as our Priest. We adore you as our God.

Resource

Catechism, 1113-1134; 1168-1185

Glossary

Liturgical Year. The celebration of the mysteries of Christ are arranged in a year-long sequence built around the most sacred three days (*Sacrum Triduum*), Holy Thursday, Good Friday, and the Easter Vigil.

Liturgy of the Hours. The public, daily prayer of the Church which prolongs the Eucharistic celebration and continues the praise of God.

Sacraments. Effective signs of grace, instituted by Christ, entrusted to the Church, by which divine life is given to us.

Life Application

1. When I receive a sacrament, do I think of Christ's presence or am I usually too distracted? What should I do to increase my awareness of Christ in the sacraments? What is different now in my participation in a sacrament compared to ten years ago?

2. Have I thought of praying morning and evening prayer from the Liturgy of the Hours? Why would it be of spiritual value to me and the Church to do so? Why is it important to praise God?

3. Which liturgical season do I like best — Advent, Christmas, Lent, or Easter? What is the attraction in each season? Why does the Church say that Holy Thursday, Good Friday, and the Easter Vigil are the most important days in the Church year?

Focus

All liturgical events are a composite of the transcendent and the immanent, that is, divine and human elements. The transcendent side draws our attention to God's presence and work. The immanent aspect turns our eyes to the human presence and its work. At liturgy God comes to us in the glory of his presence and the power of his grace. At worship people come before the Lord in awe and adoration with hearts open to the possibilities of human enrichment.

Which factor deserves the primacy? Transcendence. The essential event at liturgy is the divine presence that calls forth human reverence and awe. The second movement is that of divine grace responding to human need. The initial action then is God coming to us, to whom we respond in faith. The next action is the opening of our hearts to him, to which he responds with love and grace.

Chapter 33

Baptism – Born of Water and the Spirit

The Sacraments of Christian initiation — Baptism, Confirmation, and the Eucharist — lay the foundations of every Christian life.

Catechism, 1212

Pioneer liturgist Monsignor Martin Hellriegel loved to tell a story about an experience he had in returning to his native Germany. He was sipping coffee in a Bremen train station when a young man came up to him to sell him a newspaper. Hellriegel asked him where he was from. "Father, I am from Vienna, but I found my Lord Jesus Christ in Bremen." Stirred by this faith sharing, Hellriegel went to his parish church before going home. He knelt before the baptismal font and said with gratitude, "Here I found my Lord Jesus Christ."

Baptism initiates us into the life of the Spirit, union with Christ, and membership in the Church. This sacrament makes possible our reception of the other sacraments. We should always connect Baptism with (1) Water, (2) Spirit, and (3) Light.

Baptism means being plunged or immersed in water. The candidate is "buried" (dies to sin) and "rises" to the new life of grace. Read St. Paul's explanation of this in Romans 6:1-5.

Baptism is a bath of regeneration in the Holy Spirit. This sacrament signifies and accomplishes rebirth in water and the Spirit, so we can enter God's kingdom (Jn 3:5).

Third, Baptism is called enlightenment because the baptized receive catechetical instruction about God's self-revelation and saving work in history.

The process of becoming a Christian includes several stages. The Rite of Christian Initiation of Adults best illustrates this. The rituals include proclamation of the Word, acceptance of the Gospel through faith and conversion, the profession of faith, and the three Sacraments of Initiation: Baptism, Confirmation, and Eucharist. As a catechizing and celebrating community, the parish walks with the candidates in this journey. In the Baptism of infants, the parents are led through a preparation process.

The vivid rituals associated with this process of initiation of adults are powerful learning experiences: the sign of the Cross, proclamation of the Word, catechetical instruction, exorcism, profession of faith, baptismal water and font, the candle, immersion or pouring of water (Baptism), white garment, saying the Our Father, anointing with perfumed oil (Confirmation), celebration of Eucharist and First Communion — all in the context of a supporting parish faith community.

Testimony about the baptizing of infants dates back to the second century. Most likely, babies were baptized in apostolic times when whole households were brought into the faith (Acts 16:15). Godparents and the whole parish community should help parents in developing the graces received in Baptism by both babies and adults.

In Baptism, all sins are forgiven, original sin and all personal sin and any temporal punishment due to sin. But human weakness remains and the newly baptized must embark on a journey of faith growth, moral improvement, and spiritual development. This "new creation" will have the power of the Spirit to do this.

Reflection

1. *What are the names and effects of Baptism?*

   Baptism is an immersion in water where we die and rise with Christ. It is a bath of regeneration in the Holy Spirit. It is an enlightenment communicating God's saving Revelation to the candidate.

   By Baptism all sins are forgiven, original sin and all personal sins, as well as all punishment for sin (cf. *Catechism*, 1214-1216; 1263).

2. *What are the Sacraments of Initiation?*

   "The sacraments of Christian initiation [are] Baptism, Confirmation, and the Eucharist . . ." (*Catechism*, 1212; the process of initiation is described in the *Catechism*, 1234-1245).

3. *How necessary is Baptism?*

   "The Lord himself affirms that Baptism is necessary for salvation (Jn 3:5)" (*Catechism*, 1257; for the Church's teaching about the salvation of those to whom Baptism has not been preached, read the full exposition of *Catechism*, 1257-1261).

Prayer

We praise you, O God, for our Baptism in the name of the Father, and of the Son, and of the Holy Spirit.

Resource

Catechism, 1210-1284

Glossary

Baptism. A sacrament whereby we are immersed in water to die to sin and rise with Christ; we are bathed in the Holy Spirit to be regenerated in grace; we are enlightened by God's Revelation. Baptism frees us from original sin, actual sin, and the temporal punishment due to sin.

Catechumenate. Another name for the RCIA process.

Confirmation. Confirmation perfects the grace of Baptism. It is the sacrament which gives the Holy Spirit to root us more profoundly in the divine filiation, incorporates us more profoundly in Christ, renders more solidly our connection with the Church, associates us with the Church's mission, and helps us witness Christian faith by words and works (cf. *Catechism*, 1316).

Eucharist. The Eucharist is the heart and summit of the life of the Church, for in it Christ associates his Church and all its members in his sacrifice of praise and act of thanks once and for all on the Cross to the Father. By this sacrifice he obtains the graces of salvation for his Body which is the Church (cf. *Catechism*, 1407).

RCIA. The initials for Rite of Christian Initiation of Adults. This is a process for introducing converts into communion with the Catholic Church in the sacraments of Baptism, Confirmation, and Eucharist.

Sacraments of Initiation. These are Baptism, Confirmation, and Eucharist.

Life Application

1. I am used to celebrating my birthday. How should I celebrate my baptismal day? Every Easter we renew our baptismal vows. What is the value of renewing our faith commitment to Christ and the Church?

2. Have I been involved in an RCIA process? From what I know about it, why is the involvement of the parish community important? The proclamation of the Scriptures and the response of faith and conversion model for me what I should do regularly. How does this benefit me?

3. Converts remind cradle Catholics about the value of faith. What steps am I taking to undergo lifelong conversion to Christ?

Focus

Membership in the Church is not like getting an academic degree — once you've gotten it, it's all over and there is no more that needs to be done. Rather, membership in the Church is like joining a family. Once you have joined, your responsibilities have just begun.

The Spirit is alive in the Church today as the Spirit was alive in the past, and one of the ways we perceive the life of the Spirit is in the gift of faith that is constantly being given to the new members of the Church. We need to know that this Church of ours is alive and well, and the catechumenate is one of the ways that good news reaches us.

Archbishop Daniel Pilarczyk

Chapter 34

Confirmation
– Becoming a Courageous Catholic

For "by the sacrament of Confirmation, [the baptized] are more perfectly bound to the Church and are enriched with a special strength of the Holy Spirit. Hence they are, as true witnesses of Christ, more strictly obliged to spread and defend the faith by word and deed" (*Lumen Gentium*, 11)

Catechism, 1285

In April 1991, six million Ukrainian Catholics arose from the "tomb" of seventy years of persecution by the Communist state. Thousands flocked to St. Yuri's Cathedral in Lvov for the first Catholic Mass of the Resurrection to be celebrated there in decades. These courageous Catholics had no other reason to stay with Christ and the Church but their faith.

The culture and the state tried to destroy them by every modern means of extinction: murder, prison, beatings, intimidation, social ostracism, denial of higher education, refusal of good jobs, ridicule, propaganda. The grace of the Spirit and the faith of the people prevailed.

These living martyrs of our Church best exemplify the intended power of Confirmation – or Chrismation, as it is called in the Eastern Churches. The intimidation and hostility to Catholicism in Western culture is more subtle, but just as real. The purification of Catholicism in the West means that only supernatural faith and God's grace will work. People will remain witnessing Catholics because they believe. That's it. That is what our Confirmation calling is all about.

What is the Sacrament of Confirmation? The *Catechism* (see 1293-1300) sets out the rite and celebration of the sacrament, from which we best learn its significance. It is the second of the three Sacraments of Initiation. In this sacrament, we receive a special giving of the Holy Spirit.

Normally, the bishop confers the sacrament, but at times it is done by a priest. In the Western Church, the sacrament is conferred by anointing of Holy Chrism (oil) on the forehead, done while imposing the hand, with these words, "Be sealed with the gift of the Holy Spirit."

In the Eastern Churches, the principal parts of the body are anointed with myron (in Greek, meaning "sweet oil"): the forehead, eyes, nose, ears, lips, chest, hands, and feet. Each anointing is accompanied by the formula, "The seal of the gift of the Holy Spirit" (*Catechism*, 1300).

The principal effect of Confirmation/Chrismation is the pouring forth of the Holy Spirit in his fullness. We are more deeply united to God as "*Abba*, Father." We are joined more firmly to Christ. We experience a richer outpouring of the gifts of the Spirit. We are more perfectly bound to the Church.

Both Baptism and Confirmation confer a "character" — a permanent spiritual mark of identity with Christ. Because of the permanence of this character, we cannot receive either Baptism or Confirmation again. Baptismal character marks us as a disciple of Christ. Confirmational character marks us as public witnesses to Christ.

Because of the secularization of Western culture, Confirmation has become more truly the "Sacrament of Courage" and Christian witnessing. As we mature in our faith, we realize more and more clearly why it takes so much faith to be a Catholic.

Reflection

1. *What is the Sacrament of Confirmation?*
   "In the Latin rite, 'the sacrament of Confirmation is conferred through the anointing with chrism on the forehead, which is done by the laying on of the hand, and through the words: . . . [Be sealed with the Gift of the Holy Spirit]' " (*Catechism*, 1300).

2. *What are the effects of Confirmation?*
   We more clearly say, "*Abba*, Father." We come closer to Christ and experience an increase of the gifts of the Spirit. Our tie to the Church is stronger. The Spirit helps us spread and defend our faith by word and deed as witnesses of Christ (cf. *Catechism*, 1302-1303).

3. *Explain the three sacramental anointings.*
   Baptismal anointing signifies purification. The Anointing of the Sick points to healing and consolation. Confirmation anointing is a sign of consecration (cf. *Catechism*, 1294).

Prayer

Come, Holy Spirit, with your gifts and strength. Help us share and defend our faith as strong witnesses to Christ.

Resource

Catechism, 1285-1321

Glossary

Character. A spiritual mark of identity with Christ received in the Sacraments of Baptism, Confirmation, and Holy Orders. The character also signifies these sacraments can only be received once.

Chrismation. The name for Confirmation in Eastern Rite Catholic Churches.

Confirmation. A sacrament in which a bishop or priest anoints us with oil, imposes his hands, and says, "Be sealed with the gift of the Holy Spirit."

Life Application

1. What do I remember about my Confirmation? What are some challenges I have faced in remaining loyal to my faith? How would I handle those challenges differently today?

2. How conscious am I that my body is a temple of the Holy Spirit? Some people speak of their bodies in terms of "temple maintenance," meaning care of the spiritual, physical, and moral aspects of their bodies. How am I doing on "temple maintenance"?

3. Today's culture upholds many values contrary to the teachings of Christ and the Church. What are some of these false positions and how am I witnessing my Confirmation vows by courageously practicing Christ's teachings?

Focus

St. Thomas More witnessed his Confirmation commitment to the point of being martyred for his faith.

He refused to acknowledge King Henry VIII's divorce or his becoming head of the Church of England. He did this risking his life and financial disaster for his family, who were not pleased with him on this matter.

The most interesting feature of his decision was that practically every leader in England, lay and clerical (with very few exceptions), gave in to the king. Like any Renaissance humanist he was ready to jibe at the follies of bishops, but he remained loyal to the universal Church when they and the theologians turned away from the Church's teachings on divorce and the authority of the pope as the real head of the Church. What made him do this? The grace of the Holy Spirit and his determination to be a man of moral principle.

He retained his patience and good humor to the end, advising the executioner not to touch his beard "for it had done no harm." And then on a more serious note, he said, "Be not afraid. You send me to God."

Chapter 35

Eucharist – The Supper of the Lamb

The holy Eucharist completes Christian initiation.

Catechism, 1322

In pre-Judaic times, shepherds celebrated the birth of the spring lambs by sacrificing the firstborn lamb to a god. They saved a portion from their altar and feasted on the remainder of the lamb. Farmers commemorated the spring harvest by offering the first sheaves of barley to a god. They saved some of the sacrifice and made unleavened bread for a meal. They connected altar and table, sacrifice and meal, offering and communion.

The Jewish people adopted these festivals as historical and religious feasts for three reasons: (1) to thank God for salvation from the slavery of Egypt and other blessings; (2) to pray for fertility of their families, flocks, and farms; and (3) to ask God for unity in their families and tribes.

These festivals of Passover and Unleavened Bread were the background of the Lord's Supper on the first Holy Thursday. Jesus changed two of the rituals that evening. He took the unleavened bread, which was normally shared in silence, blessed it, broke it, and gave it to the apostles, saying, "Take and eat. This is my body, which will be broken for you. Do this in memory of me."

He took the third cup of wine after the meal, which was usually a joyful, silent toast, and said, "Take and drink. This is the cup of my blood, the blood of the new and eternal covenant, which will be shed for you. Do this in memory of me."

The Last Supper looked to the *past* and gave new meaning to Passover. It also embraced the *future* – the Passion and Resurrection. Sacramentally, the events of Good Friday and Easter were made present. Passover and Passion illumine Eucharist. The sacrificial altar of Good Friday and the Communion table of Holy Thursday become one reality.

What is the Sacrament of the Eucharist? The many names we give to this holy mystery of salvation outline its rich meaning.

Eucharist, because we thank God for gifts and graces.

Lord's Supper, because it is a sacred meal of a divine and human community, continuing what happened on Holy Thursday.

Breaking of Bread, the first Christian term for Eucharist.

Holy Sacrifice, for it makes Christ's sacrifice present.

Divine Liturgy, for all liturgy finds its center and expression in the Eucharistic celebration.

Eucharistic Assembly, for the assembly of the faithful celebrate it as the visible expression of the Church.

Holy Communion, for the Body of Christ feeds and advances the Body of Christ, the Church, through Communion.

Mass, for the faithful are sent forth to do God's will.

For an explanation of the Eucharistic celebration, read the *Catechism*, 1345-1355. The Eucharist is "the source and summit of the Christian life" (*Lumen Gentium*, 11; SVC). "The Eucharist . . . signifies and wonderfully effects [the] sharing in God's life and [the] unity of God's people by which the Church exists" (*Eucharisticum Mysterium*, 6; SVC). "For in the most blessed Eucharist is contained the whole spiritual good of the Church, namely, Christ. . ." (*Presbyterorum Ordinis*, 5; SVC).

From the sun comes the light by which we can see everything. From the Eucharist flows the light by which we perceive the mystery of God. Eat this Bread and you shall never be hungry. Drink this Cup and you shall never thirst.

Reflection

1. *What happens at the Eucharistic celebration?*
   "The Eucharistic celebration always includes: the proclamation of the Word of God; thanksgiving to God the Father for all his benefits, above all the gift of his Son; the consecration of bread and wine; and participation in the liturgical banquet by receiving the Lord's body and blood. These elements constitute one single act of worship" (*Catechism*, 1408).

2. *What are the essential signs of Eucharist?*
   "The essential signs of the Eucharistic sacrament are wheat bread and grape wine, on which the blessing of the Holy Spirit is invoked and the priest pronounces the words of consecration spoken by Jesus during the Last Supper . . ." (*Catechism*, 1412).

3. *Who may preside at the Eucharist?*
   "Only validly ordained priests can preside at the Eucharist and consecrate the bread and the wine so that they become the Body and Blood of the Lord" (*Catechism*, 1411).

4. *What is the obligation to attend Sunday Mass?*
   "The Church obliges the faithful to take part in the Divine Liturgy on Sundays and feast days and, prepared by the sacrament of Reconciliation, to receive the Eucharist at least once a year, if possible during the Easter season" (*Catechism*, 1389).

Prayer

Jesus, my Lord, my God, my all, how can I love you as I ought? Or how do I revere this wondrous gift, so far surpassing hope or thought? I adore you. Make me love you more and more.

Resource

Catechism, 1322-1419

Glossary

Eucharist. A sacramental celebration in which (a) the Word of God is proclaimed and responded to in faith; (b) the priest consecrates the bread and wine which are turned into the Body and Blood of Christ by the power of the Holy Spirit; and (c) the worshipers receive Communion in this sacred banquet.

Lord's Supper. The Holy Eucharist is a Breaking of the Bread, a sacred meal in which a divine and human community participate. It remembers and makes present the first Eucharist on Holy Thursday.

Sacrifice of the Mass. The Holy Eucharist makes present the redeeming sacrifice of Christ at Calvary and the saving Resurrection of Jesus at Easter.

Life Application

1. When did I receive my First Communion? What do I remember best about it? How do I prepare for Mass today? What features of the present liturgy of the Eucharist best help my faith to develop?

2. The *Catechism* gives eight names to describe the richness of the mystery of the Eucharist. They are listed in the opening section of this chapter. Read them again. Why is it important that I keep in mind all the descriptions to have an adequate appreciation of the Eucharist?

3. If I were denied access to the Eucharist, would it make a difference in my life? If I had lived in Russia during the persecution of believers, how do I think I would have kept my faith?

Focus

[Jesus] declared that the chalice, which comes from his creation, was his blood and he makes it the nourishment of our blood. He affirmed that the bread, which comes from his creation, was his body, and he makes it the nourishment of our body. When the chalice we mix and the bread we bake receive the word of God, the eucharistic elements become the body and blood of Christ, by which our bodies live and grow. . . .

The slip of a vine planted in the ground bears fruit at the proper time. The grain of wheat falls into the ground and decays only to be raised up again and multiplied by the Spirit of God who sustains all things. The Wisdom of God places these things at the service of man and when they receive God's word they become the eucharist, which is the body and blood of Christ. In the same way our bodies, which have been nourished by the eucharist, will be buried in the earth and will decay, but they will rise again at the appointed time, for the Word of God will raise them up to the glory of God the Father.

St. Irenaeus in the *Liturgy of the Hours*

Chapter 36

How Real Is the Real Presence?

"This presence is called 'real' — by which it is not intended to exclude the other types of presence . . . but because it is presence in the fullest sense: that is to say, it is a *substantial* presence by which Christ, God and man, makes himself wholly and entirely present" (Pope Paul VI, *Mysterium Fidei*, 39).

Catechism, 1374

An Irish nun, Sister Briege McKenna, has a worldwide healing and spiritual ministry to priests. She says, "I could not do this without spending three hours a day before the Blessed Sacrament." Similarly, Mother Teresa and her sisters draw strength for their service to the poorest of the poor from the Mass and adoration of the Real Presence of Jesus in the Eucharist.

Mother Angelica attributes the effectiveness of her television and short-wave radio ministry to the graces that come from the perpetual adoration of the Eucharist by her and her sisters at their monastery in Birmingham.

Chapter six of John's Gospel records Christ's dialogue at the Capernaum synagogue about the Bread of Life (Jn 6:22-71). He had recently performed the "bread miracle" and fed five thousand people. He filled them with natural bread.

Now he promised to nourish them with supernatural bread. Eight times he told them he was the living bread come down from heaven. Four times he insisted they must eat his flesh and drink his blood in order to have eternal life here and hereafter.

At first they thought he was speaking metaphorically. But Jesus emphasized and repeated his teaching. They asked disbelievingly, "How can this man give us his flesh to eat"? Jesus did not soften his words. He did not correct misunderstandings. He meant what he said and they knew it. "For my flesh is true food, and my blood is true drink" (v. 55).

Many of his listeners were disciples. They were used to his miracles and mysterious sayings. They could not accept him. He told them to think spiritually. "Does this shock you? . . . It is the spirit that gives life" (vs. 61, 63). They left him. Then he faced his apostles. "Do you also want to leave?" Peter said, "Master, to whom shall we go? . . . We have come to believe . . . you are the Holy One of God" (vs. 68-69). The text says that Judas did not believe. It was on the issue of the Eucharist that he abandoned Christ. This is the clearest example in the Gospel of someone rejecting Jesus over a doctrinal matter.

The Fathers of the Church all affirmed the Real Presence of Jesus in the Eucharist. St. Athanasius says, "After the great prayers, the bread is the Body and the wine is the Blood of Jesus." Since the Middle Ages, the Church has called the process by which this comes about *transubstantiation*. By the power of the Spirit and the words of the priest, the bread and wine are changed into the Body, Blood, Soul, and Divinity of Jesus Christ. The bread and wine still look the same, but their reality has changed. Faith alone can see and believe this.

We reserve the Eucharist in the tabernacle both for Communion for the sick and an opportunity for adoration and meditation by the faithful. St. John Vianney, who loved to sit before the tabernacle, recalled the words of a pious parishioner: "I look at Jesus and he looks at me." This powerful devotion increases our love for the Mass and the effectiveness of our service to family, friends, and community.

Reflection

1. *What does the Council of Trent say about Real Presence?*
   " '. . . by the consecration of the bread and wine there takes place a change of the whole substance of the bread into the substance of the body of Christ our Lord and of the whole substance of the wine into the substance of his blood' (Council of Trent)" (*Catechism*, 1376).

2. *What is the basis for reserving the Eucharist?*
   "The Eucharistic presence of Christ begins at the moment of the consecration and endures as long as the Eucharistic species subsist" (*Catechism*, 1377).

3. *What is the value of Eucharistic devotion?*
   ". . . [Jesus] wanted us to have the memorial of the love with which he loved us 'to the end (Jn 13:1)'. . . . In his Eucharistic presence he remains mysteriously in our midst as one who loved us and gave himself up for us 'The Church and the world have a great need for Eucharistic worship. Jesus awaits us in this sacrament of love. Let us not refuse the time to go to meet him in adoration, in contemplation full of faith, and open to making amends for the serious offenses and crimes of the world' (Pope John Paul II, *Dominicae Cenae*, 3)" (*Catechism*, 1380).

Prayer

Eucharistic Jesus, I adore you with all my heart. Under these visible signs you are really present. In contemplating you, all else fades away. Increase my love of you, others, and self.

Resource

Catechism, 1373-1381

Glossary

Corpus Christi. Latin words meaning "Body of Christ." The feast of Corpus Christi occurs on the Sunday after Trinity Sunday.

Real Presence. After the bread and wine are consecrated at Mass, they become the Body, Blood, Soul, and Divinity of Jesus Christ. We know this with faith. This Real Presence of Jesus is reserved in our tabernacles in our parish churches for our adoration and devotion, and for Communion for the sick.

Transubstantiation. Refers to the process of change of substances that takes place in the bread and wine at Mass when they become the Real Presence of Jesus.

Life Application

1. When I enter my parish church, how do I acknowledge the Real Presence of Jesus, whether it be in the main body of the church or in the Blessed Sacrament chapel? What signs of reverence, adoration, and devotion are most fitting?

2. How often do I make a special visit to the Blessed Sacrament for a few minutes, a half hour, or an hour of adoration? Why is this important for the growth of my faith and the deepening of my spiritual life?

3. How do I help my family and others to cultivate a devotion to the Blessed Sacrament? Saints and other devoted Catholics have always known the value of the Real Presence. What do they know that I have yet to find out?

Focus

As a Catholic, what seems to have struck Newman [the Anglican convert, John Henry Cardinal Newman] more than anything else about the worship of the Catholic Church was devotion to the reserved sacrament. Shortly after he [became a Catholic], he wrote enthusiastically to a friend, "It is such an incomprehensible blessing to have Christ in bodily presence in one's house, within one's walls, as swallows up all other privileges. . . . To know that He is close by — to be able again and again through the day to go in to Him." So strongly did he feel this that he could say, "Now after tasting of the awful delight of worshipping God in His Temple, how unspeakably cold is the idea of a Temple without that Divine Presence! One is tempted to say what is the meaning, what is the use of it?" The sacrament reserved in the tabernacle was not simply a source of spiritual comfort, but it was what above all helped to produce "the deep impression of religion as an objective fact."

Ian Ker, *Newman: On Being a Christian*

Chapter 37

Forgiveness Heals People

The Lord Jesus Christ, physician of our souls and bodies . . . has willed that his Church continue, in the power of the Holy Spirit, his work of healing and salvation. . . .

Catechism, 1421

The Sacraments of Initiation give us new life in Christ. But our new life is threatened by sin. Moreover, sickness and death affect us all. Jesus, our divine physician, has given the Church the sacraments of healing — Reconciliation, and the Anointing of the Sick — to forgive sins and help the sick and the dying.

The Sacrament of Reconciliation involves a conversion of ourselves to God; a confession of sins to a priest; a penance process of moral change; a reconciliation to God, others, and self; and the forgiveness of our sins.

Lifelong conversion to God, by moral and spiritual growth, is the key to understanding and profiting from this sacrament. It assumes a frank acknowledgement of the reality of sin and of our own sinfulness. The Holy Spirit helps us in this by: (1) *convincing* us of our sinfulness, (2) *convicting* us like a divine lawyer, (3) *converting* us to grace and love, and (4) *consoling* us in the process (Jn 16:8-9).

God alone forgives sins. Jesus, however, conferred on his apostles and their successors, the bishops, the power to forgive sins (cf. Mt 16:19; 18:18; 28:16-20). Priests share in this power. In this sacrament we are not only reconciled to God, but also to the Church community as well as to ourselves.

This sacrament always has two characteristics: first, the acts of the penitent converted by the Spirit: contrition, confession, and satisfaction; second, the acts of the Church through the bishops and priests. They offer, in the name of Jesus, forgiveness of sins, the manner of satisfaction, prayer for the sinners, and they do penance with them.

For those who commit mortal sin after Baptism, this sacrament is necessary for recovering friendship with God and reconciliation with the Church community.

The penitent should have sorrow for sins. This means turning away from evil and converting to God. When love of God is the motive for doing this, we have perfect contrition. When other motives, such as disgust about the sin or fear of hell, bring us to confession, that is called *imperfect contrition*. The Spirit moves us in both instances and initiates our conversion.

Penitents, who have reached the age of reason, should confess all grave, mortal sins committed after Baptism. While it is not strictly necessary to confess venial sins and faults, it is helpful to do so for the training of conscience and to make progress in our lives in the Spirit. Penitents should then perform the penance given by the priest. This helps purify our souls and liberate us from the "temporal punishment" due to sin. The Church's teachings about indulgences is pertinent here. Read the *Catechism* 1471-1479 on this teaching.

Parishes offer confession face-to-face with the priest or in an anonymous manner where the penitent confesses behind a screen. There are also penance services at various times during the year when there is a Proclamation of the Word, a homily, prayers, and music to help people appreciate the sacrament's purpose. These services are accompanied by individual confessions to the priest. In emergency situations, General Absolution may be given. If the penitent was in mortal sin, that sin should be confessed at a later time to the priest.

All sacraments bring the participants divine joy and peace. The special happiness received here arises from lifting the burden of sin and guilt. We are released to the freedom of grace. We are restored to friendship with God, others, and self.

Reflection

1. *How are sins committed after Baptism forgiven?*
   "The forgiveness of sins committed after Baptism is conferred by a particular sacrament called the sacrament of conversion, confession, penance, or reconciliation" (*Catechism*, 1486).

2. *What does conversion to God imply?*
   "The movement of return to God, called conversion and repentance, entails sorrow for and abhorrence of sins committed, and the firm purpose of sinning no more in the future" (*Catechism*, 1490; cf. 1450-1458).

3. *What are some effects of the Sacrament of Reconciliation?*
   The spiritual effects of the Sacrament of Reconciliation are: reconciliation with God and the Church; peace of conscience and spiritual comfort; partial remission of the temporal punishment due to sin; increase of spiritual power for the Christian struggle; remission of the eternal punishment incurred by mortal sins (cf. *Catechism*, 1496).

Prayer

O God, be merciful to me, a sinner. Take away my pride and give me your humility. Remove my greed and give me your simplicity of life. Replace my anger with your joy. Turn my envy into your generosity. Convert my laziness into your enthusiasm. Transform my obsessions into your moderateness. Take away my lust and give me your divine purity.

Resource

Catechism, 1420-1498

Glossary

Acts of the Church in Confession. Bishops and priests, acting in the name of Jesus Christ and the Church, offer forgiveness of sins, penance, prayer for sinners, and they do penance with them.

Acts of the Penitent in Confession. Contrition, confession, satisfaction.

Perfect and Imperfect Contrition. Perfect contrition arises from the love of God. Imperfect contrition results from other motives such as disgust of the sin or fear of hell. The Holy Spirit motivates us in both cases.

Sacrament of Reconciliation. Also called the Sacrament of Penance, conversion, and confession, it is the sacrament in which the sins committed after Baptism are forgiven. It involves a reconciliation to God, others, and self.

Life Application

1. How much do I value the Sacrament of Reconciliation? What evidence have I to show for this? How different is my confessional practice today from ten years ago? If there is a great difference, positive or negative, why the change?

2. The seven capital sins afflict most people more or less intensely. They are: pride, greed, anger, lust, gluttony, envy, and laziness. As I ponder this list, what areas need to be fought against? How can regular confession help me?

3. If I have an antipathy to confession, how can I overcome it? Who can help me with this? How did the problem arise? What are some positive experiences of confession that will help me?

Focus

Our Lord Jesus Christ reconciled God and [mankind] through the mystery of his death and resurrection. This ministry of reconciliation was committed to the Church through the apostles by our Lord (2 Cor. 5:18) and the Church has executed the commission by bearing the glad tidings of salvation to [all peoples] and by baptizing them in water and the Holy Spirit (see Matt. 28:19).

Because of human weakness, however, it happens that Christians "abandon the love they had at first" . . . and by sinning break the links of friendship that bind them to God. For this reason the Lord instituted a special sacrament for the remission of sins committed after Baptism (see John 20:21-23). The Church has celebrated this sacrament through the ages, in various ways indeed, but always retaining its essential elements.

The Church has it at heart to call the faithful to continual conversion and renewal.

Pope Paul VI, *The New Order of Penance*; SVC

Chapter 38

Is There Anyone Sick Among You?

"By the sacred anointing of the sick and the prayer of the priests the whole Church commends those who are ill to the suffering and glorified Lord, that he may raise them up and save them" (*Lumen Gentium*, 11).

Catechism, 1499

A priest went to a farmhouse to bring the Anointing of the Sick to an elderly lady. Only her husband was with her. The doctor was delayed. Her breathing came in great gasps and she seemed like she would soon die. After the anointing, the priest prayed with the couple and departed. Three weeks later she was up and around and attending church.

The Anointing of the Sick is not always followed by a recovery from illness, but sometimes this does occur. The anointing reflects Christ's healing ministry. Almost all the miracles of Jesus are acts of healing an illness or affliction. Three times he raised someone from the dead. He connected this ministry with a call to faith. Jesus also healed the souls of people by forgiving their sins. At the same time, he used his own sufferings and death to redeem us from sin and give us divine life.

The Holy Spirit gives to certain saints and other members of the Church the charism of healing. Yet all the sick are not cured despite fervent prayer. St. Paul learned why from Christ. "My grace is sufficient for you, for power is made perfect in weakness" (2 Cor 12:9). Our pain can be redemptive. "I rejoice in my sufferings for your sake, and in my flesh I am filling up what is lacking in the afflictions of Christ on behalf of his body, which is the Church" (Col 1:24). This approach gives meaning to suffering.

In the Sacrament of the Anointing of the Sick, oil blessed by the bishop is used. The practice dates from the instruction of James. "Is anyone among you sick? He should summon the presbyters of the church, and they should pray over him and anoint [him] with oil in the name of the Lord" (Jas 5:14).

The Church celebrates this sacrament for those who begin to be — or actually are — in danger of death. Vatican II says, "Hence, as soon as anyone of the faithful begins to be in danger of death from sickness or old age, the fitting time . . . to receive this sacrament has . . . arrived" (*Sacrosanctum Concilium*, 73; SVC).

What are the effects of this sacrament? The Holy Spirit gives sick people a renewal of confidence in God, comfort to cope with illness, union with Christ's Passion so as to participate in his saving work. In the celebration, the Church, through the Communion of Saints, prays for the sick, who in turn contribute to the sanctification of other members of the community.

For those sick people who are on their final journey into the next life, this is an anointing unto glory, a sacrament of departure. It prepares them to meet God. Baptism began conforming them to the death and Resurrection of Christ. This sacrament completes that work. The sick may also receive the Eucharist, called *Viaticum*. The word means that Christ is "with us on the way" through his Eucharistic presence and power.

It is often said the dying go through stages of denial, anger, bargaining, depression, and acceptance. The Anointing of the Sick helps loved ones release the dying to God and assists the gravely ill to accept death should it be God's will at that time.

Reflection

1. *When should the Anointing of the Sick take place?*
   "The proper time for receiving this holy anointing has certainly arrived when the believer begins to be in danger of death because of illness or old age.

   "Each time a Christian falls seriously ill, he may receive the Anointing of the Sick, and also when, after he has received it, the illness worsens" (*Catechism*, 1528-1529).

2. *Who is the minister of the Holy Anointing?*
   "Only priests (presbyters and bishops) can give the sacrament of Anointing of the Sick . . ." (*Catechism*, 1530).

3. *What are the benefits of the Holy Anointing?*
   In the Anointing of the Sick, the Holy Spirit: unites the sick to the Passion of Christ for their good and that of the Church; prepares them for passage to eternal life; grants forgiveness of sins if the person is unable to receive the Sacrament of Penance; restores health if this be God's will (cf. *Catechism*, 1532).

Prayer

O Jesus, friend and healer, console and strengthen the sick and the dying. Join them to your saving work for all people.

Resource

Catechism, 1499-1532

Glossary

Sacrament of Anointing. In this sacrament, the Church, through anointing and the Spirit, prepares a gravely ill person for passage to eternal life. Sometimes health is restored, if it be God's will.

Viaticum. The name given to Communion for the dying. It comes from the Latin "with one on the way."

Life Application

1. What is my general attitude to suffering and death? Do these troubles make me angry? How do they affect my relationship with God? How do I apply the goodness, love, and power of God to the problem and mystery of suffering?
2. Am I accustomed to uniting my troubles, pain, and suffering to the Passion of Christ for the salvation of the world? How does this make sense out of suffering?
3. If I received the Sacrament of Anointing and was granted a cure of my illness, what would that do for my faith? If, on the other hand, I was looking for a cure and did not get it, what impact would that have on my faith? What is the most important aspect of the Sacrament of Anointing?

Focus

Nothing tests a family's capacity to love more than the experience of caring for a dying member. True love has always meant forgetfulness of self in order to think of the needs of others. In this case, love will involve a steady concentration on the fact that dying persons are still perfectly human. They are not acting out a role as though they have suddenly decided to be on a stage. Nor are they infants despite their helplessness. They are still Mom, Pop, Grandma, Grandpa, Son, Daughter, Brother, and Sister. The heart that loved you when it was well still loves you and pleads for love in return.

Bishops, Priests, and Deacons

> . . . Holy Orders . . . is the sacrament of apostolic ministry. It includes three degrees: episcopate, presbyterate, and diaconate.
>
> *Catechism*, 1536

In 1979, Pope John Paul II wrote the first of his annual Holy Thursday letters to priests. Addressing priestly self-confidence, he wrote, "Dear Brothers: Think of the places where for many years, people experiencing the lack of a priest, they do not cease to hope for his presence. Sometimes they meet in an abandoned shrine and place on the altar a stole which they still keep. They recite the prayers of the Eucharistic liturgy. At the moment that corresponds to transubstantiation, a deep silence comes on them, a silence sometimes broken by weeping. So deeply do they feel the priest's absence."

This precious gift of priesthood is given to the Church in the Sacrament of Holy Orders. Baptism initiates each member of the Church into the priesthood of all believers. The Sacrament of Holy Orders involves a spiritual power not given to every Catholic. Only the priest and bishop may celebrate Eucharist and the Sacrament of Reconciliation. Only the bishop ordains priests and deacons. Only bishops can ordain other bishops.

The two priesthoods differ but enrich each other. "Though they differ essentially and not only in degree, the common priesthood of the faithful and the ministerial . . . priesthood are . . . ordered one to another" (*Lumen Gentium*, 10; SVC). Christ calls the baptized to share in the Spirit's work of *sanctifying the world*. Christ calls the ordained priesthood to share in the Spirit's work of *sanctifying the faithful*.

The ordained priest acts in the *person of Christ as head of the Church*, teaching, shepherding, and sanctifying God's people. The priest also acts in the *name of the Church*, offering the Sacrifice of the Body of Christ to the Father for the salvation of God's people and the world itself. The bishop has the fullness of priesthood. Priests share in the bishops' priesthood.

Ordained priesthood is permanent. The Sacrament of Holy Orders confers a permanent priestly character. This character reflects Christ's absolute covenant with the Church. Just as Jesus never revokes his covenant with the Church, neither should the priest.

In the Western Church, the call to priesthood is connected to the call to celibacy. Only those deemed to have received the celibacy call, as well as the call to Holy Orders, can be ordained. In the Eastern Church married men may be admitted to the priesthood. Their bishops are chosen from celibate monks.

Only males can be ordained. In response to the request for women's ordination, Pope Paul VI responded, "The Church, in fidelity to the example of the Lord, does not consider herself authorized to admit women to priestly ordination."

Deacons receive the Sacrament of Holy Orders, but not priesthood. Deacons may baptize, preach, and impart liturgical blessings such as at marriages.

The Sacrament of Holy Orders does not automatically make the recipients holy. Bishops, priests, and deacons have a grave responsibility to develop a deep union with Jesus. They should practice virtues, especially humility, faith, obedience, love, care, compassion for people, and devotion to the Eucharist.

Reflection

1. *How is the Sacrament of Holy Orders conferred?*
   "The sacrament of Holy Orders is conferred by the laying on of hands followed by a solemn prayer of consecration asking God to grant the ordained the graces of the Holy Spirit required for his ministry. Ordination imprints an indelible sacramental character" (*Catechism*, 1597).

2. *What are the three degrees of the Sacrament of Holy Orders?*
   ". . . that of bishops, that of presbyters, and that of deacons" (*Catechism*, 1593). (For a fuller explanation of these degrees, see *Catechism*, 1554-1571.)

3. *What is the special characteristic of the Sacraments of Holy Orders and Marriage?*
   "Two other sacraments, Holy Orders and Matrimony, are directed towards the salvation of others; if they contribute as well to personal salvation, it is through service to others that they do so. They confer a particular mission in the Church and serve to build up the People of God" (*Catechism*, 1534).

Prayer

Lord, send us priests to serve the Church. Fill them with your Spirit. Empower them to act in the person of Christ.

Resource

Catechism, 1533-1600

Glossary

Differing Priesthoods. The baptized share in the priesthood of the faithful to sanctify the world. The ordained possess a uniquely different priesthood and it is for the sanctification of the faithful.

Priestly "Character." At ordination a spiritual character is imparted. It reflects Christ's absolute covenant with the Church. The priest is expected to reflect this covenant by fidelity to his priesthood.

Sacrament of Holy Orders. By the imposition of hands and a prayer of consecration, the Holy Spirit is invoked to ordain bishops, priests, and deacons for the sanctification of God's people.

Life Application

1. What are some stories I can tell of priests I have known who have enriched my personal and spiritual life? It is said that the celibate commitment of priests and the faithful commitment of husbands and wives in marriage can strengthen each other. What experiences have I had that demonstrate this truth?

2. What can I do to promote vocations to the priesthood? What would I say if my son told me he would like to be a priest? Similarly, how open would I be if my daughter stated she would like to enter a convent?

3. What can I do to strengthen priests in their calling? What do I want priests to do for me to strengthen me in my calling to witness Christ to the world?

Focus

The Brotherhood of Priests

There happens to be in this world of strange social conventions one friendship that transcends all conventions and knows no rules. It is the brotherhood of Catholic priests. There is not, I swear it, under the stars an intimacy more reckless or more profound than the bond between one priest and another.

It needs no coaxing, no prelude, no ritual. It is subject to no formality. We meet and possess one another instantly. There is no shadow of a barrier between us, neither age, nor antecedents, nor nationality, nor climate, nor color of skin. Ours is a blunt, rough-hewn affection.

His home is my home, his fireside, my fireside, his altar, my altar. I can give him my confidences promptly and without reserve. I can neither edify nor scandalize him. We can quarrel without offense, praise each other without flattery — sit silently and say nothing.

How and why all this can happen is our own secret. It is the secret of men who climb a lonely drawbridge, mount a narrow stair, sleep in a lofty citadel that floats a white flag. Singly we go, independent and unpossessed, establishing no generation, each a conclusion to his race and name, yet always companioning each other with strange sympathy, too tender to be called fellowship, too sturdy to be called love, but for which God will find a name when he searches our hearts in eternity.

Anonymous

Chapter 40

The Sacrament of Marriage

... this covenant between baptized persons has been raised by Christ the Lord to the dignity of a sacrament.

Catechism, 1601

The Irish have a wedding ring called the *claddagh*. It shows hands folded in prayer around a heart of love beneath a crown of fidelity. The three symbols reflect the basic virtues needed for a happy marriage and living out the expectations of the Sacrament of Marriage.

God is the author of marriage. The vocation of marriage is inscribed in the very nature of man and woman as they come forth from the hand of God. Marriage is not a purely human institution. Genesis describes the two primary purposes of marriage — conjugal love and the procreation of children.

The second creation account (Gn 2:18-25) affirms that man and woman were made for one another in a loving communion of persons. God did not want man to be alone. Hence God created woman. The man said, "This one is flesh of my flesh." The two of them became "one body." Their personal communion of love images the communion of persons in God.

God blessed the love of man and woman and destined them to be fruitful. "Be fertile and multiply" (Gn 1:28). This procreative value complements the value of conjugal love and is vital for the realization of such love. Sexual union is designed to lead to children. It also should engender spousal love. Marriage creates two benefits: spousal love and parental love.

Spousal love is called *unitive*. Parental love is *procreative*, both bearing children and raising them. The union of husband and wife is called a *contract* or a *covenant*. More powerfully, it is a *bond*. The Church teaches that the "bond" between the unitive and procreative may never be broken. This reflects God's own way of relating to us.

The Old Testament prophets often used marriage imagery to describe God's covenant with his people. He loved and created them. God never broke that bond between love and creativity. When the Son of God came to earth he continued that bond. Faithful marriage illustrates how God relates to us. Inversely, God's faithful relationship to us is a model for marriage.

Christ's first miracle was at the marriage feast of Cana (Jn 2:1-12). The Church sees great meaning in Christ's presence at this wedding. Jesus confirms the goodness of marriage. The event is a proclamation that marriage is henceforth an effective sign, a sacrament of Christ's presence. The Sacrament of Marriage celebrates the indissoluble union of bride and groom — hence no divorce. It also promises them the abundant graces of Christ to maintain the bond of conjugal love and procreative love.

The ring of fidelity, the heart of love, and the hands folded in prayer are spiritual attitudes for working through the challenges to married life in contemporary society. Religious faith will support fidelity. Union with the Holy Spirit of love will enhance conjugal and procreative love. Praying forth the power of God and each spouse's best energies will not only save marriages but make them exuberant. (In the next chapter, we will continue this reflection on the Sacrament of Marriage.)

Reflection

1. *What is implied in the marriage covenant?*
   "The marriage covenant, by which a man and a woman form with each other an intimate communion of life and love, has been founded and endowed with its own special laws by the Creator. By its very nature it is ordered to the good of the couple, as well as to the generation and education of children. Christ the Lord raised marriage between the baptized to the dignity of a sacrament" (*Catechism*, 1660).

2. *What are the essentials of marriage?*
   "Unity, indissolubility, and openness to fertility are essential to marriage" (*Catechism*, 1664).

3. *What does St. Paul say of marriage?*
   " 'Husbands, love your wives, as Christ loved the Church This is a great mystery, and I mean in reference to Christ and the Church' (Eph 5:25, 32)" (*Catechism*, 1659).

4. *In the Latin tradition, who confers the Sacrament of Matrimony?*
   "According to the Latin tradition, the spouses as ministers of Christ's grace mutually confer upon each other the sacrament of Matrimony by expressing their consent before the Church" (*Catechism*, 1623).

Prayer

O God, give all husbands and wives the strength to live in fidelity to their marriage promises to love each other and be open to begetting and rearing children. May every Christian marriage strive to reflect the absolute and loving fidelity of Christ to his Church. Fill them with abundant and lasting joy.

Resource

Catechism, 1601-1666

Glossary

Procreative Aspect of Marriage. God willed that marriage have a parental dimension in which husband and wife procreate and educate children. The bond between the unitive and procreative aspects of marriage may not be broken.

Sacrament of Marriage. Christ has elevated marriage to the dignity of a sacrament. This sacrament consecrates the covenant by which husband and wife bond themselves in a community of life and love. This sacrament is ordered to the good of the partners and the procreation and education of children.

Unitive Aspect of Marriage. God willed that husband and wife be committed permanently to each other in a communion of love. This communion of persons reflects the community of the Trinity.

Life Application

1. In my marriage I am called by God to form a communion of love with my spouse. How do we work on this challenge on a daily basis? How do differences in personality, policies about money, views of sexuality, work inside and outside the home affect our love for each other?

2. In my marriage I am called by God to procreate and educate children. How do I and my spouse respond to that call? What challenges from the culture affect our attitude toward children and the ideals we have for our children? What are the essential things we know we must do for our children?

3. What role do fidelity, love, and prayer play in our daily married life? In what way does God's fidelity to us help us to be faithful to each other?

Focus

The body is essential for communication. No body — no communication. How else could we speak to each other? What would husbands and wives do were there no body to caress? What would cheer us were there no smiles or laughter? What would touch us if we never heard a song, felt the thrill of a dance, gazed at the stars, or prayed in a cathedral? We need a body for such everyday matters. The Son of God thought enough about the body to acquire one from the Virgin Mary.

Sexuality within marriage shares in this positive view of the body. As a means of communication, marital sex sends a powerful message to the spouses involved in such intimacy. It says the self is worthwhile and a center of dignity. Human sex is inseparable from the person. Animals have instinctive sex. Humans have interpersonal sex. It discloses both the depth of the bond they have with each other and that which God has with them.

Chapter 41

Marriage Is Forever

"God himself is the author of marriage" (*Gaudium et Spes*, 48)

Catechism, 1603

The book of Tobit tells the story of Sarah, whose first seven husbands all died on their wedding night. They wanted sex without love, marriage without reference to God's will for marriage.

Young Tobit became her eighth husband. He understood that sexuality should be ordered to conjugal and procreative love as God planned. On their wedding night they first devoted themselves to a prayerful reflection on the meaning of marriage and sexuality. This attitude of faith saved the life of Tobit and assured the future of their marriage.

Tobit's prayer captures the moment: " 'Blessed are you, O God of our fathers . . . / Now Lord, you know that I take this wife of mine, / not because of lust, / but for a noble purpose. / Call down your mercy on me and on her, / and allow us to live together to a happy old age.' They said together, 'Amen, amen,' and went to bed for the night" (Tb 8:5, 7-9).

The *Catechism* teaches that Christ's graces in the Sacrament of Marriage protects three blessings or goods: (1) unity and indissolubility; (2) the fidelity of conjugal love; (3) openness to fecundity and the good of children.

The goods of unity and fidelity are destroyed by divorce. In obedience to the sixth and ninth commandments and to the very nature of marriage itself, the Church teaches that these goods require that sexuality be confined to marriage. Hence adultery and fornication are forbidden. The bond between unitive and procreative love is inseparable. Hence acts not open to creating new life such as artificial contraception and homosexual behavior violate the bond.

A strong marriage creates the possibility of a strong family. "In what might be regarded as the domestic church, the parents, by word and example, are the first heralds of the faith with regard to their children. They must foster the vocation which is proper to each child, and this with special care if it is to be religion" (*Lumen Gentium*, 11; SVC).

"The home is the first school of Christian life and a school for human enrichment" (*Gaudium et Spes*, 48; SVC). In this domestic church one learns love, the joy of work, perseverance, how to forgive, how to pray, and to participate in divine worship by the offering of one's life.

Jesus clearly blessed married life. He also blessed virginity. Jesus is the center of every Christian life. The bond with Christ precedes all other bonds, whether of family or society. The bonds of flesh do not constitute the family of Christ so much as doing God's will (Mk 3:31-35). From the beginning of the Church, men and women have renounced the good of marriage to follow the Lamb wherever he goes (Rv 14:4). Jesus himself modeled this calling and invited certain people to follow him on this path (Mt 19:12).

Consecrated virginity and celibacy do not devalue marriage. In fact the fidelity of married people encourages celibate commitment and, conversely, faithful celibate witness enriches marital fidelity.

The Sacrament of Marriage offers to the spouses the grace of Christ; he abides with them. He strengthens them to follow him in taking up their crosses, to rise after their falls through the grace of forgiveness, to forgive each other, to bear each other's burdens and fulfill the Gospel of Christ. Such couples blossom in the sunlight of fidelity and love. Marriage becomes one of life's greatest satisfactions and a foretaste of the marriage feast of the Lamb in heaven.

Reflection

1. *What are the three goods of marriage?*
   The three goods of marriage are unity and indissolubility, the fidelity of conjugal love, and openness to fecundity and the raising of children (cf. *Catechism*, 1644, 1646, 1652).

2. *Why is the Christian home called a domestic church?*
   "The Christian home is the place where children receive the first proclamation of the faith. For this reason the family home is rightly called 'the domestic church,' a community of grace and prayer, a school of human virtues and of Christian charity" (*Catechism*, 1666).

3. *How does the grace of the sacrament help spouses?*
   ". . . the grace of the sacrament [of Marriage] thus perfects the human love of the spouses, strengthens their indissoluble unity, and sanctifies them on the way to eternal life" (*Catechism*, 1661).

Prayer

Jesus, bridegroom of the Church, enrich married couples with the blessings of marriage. Strengthen their fidelity to each other. Crown their love. Envelop them in prayer. Give them joy in each other and in their children. Lead them to heaven.

Resource

Catechism, 1601-1666

Glossary

Domestic Church. The name that Vatican II gave to the Christian family. The home is the first school of Christian life and a school for human enrichment (see *Gaudium et Spes*, 47-52; SVC).

Goods of Marriage. The three goods of marriage are: (1) unity and indissolubility; (2) fidelity to conjugal love; (3) openness to fecundity and the good of children.

Virginity and Celibacy. Consecrated virginity and celibacy, normally lived in the priesthood and religious life, is a call from God to witness the reality of the kingdom and our supernatural life and destiny.

Life Application

1. Sex should be confined to marriage. How would I feel if I knew my spouse was committing adultery? What would I think if my children were engaged in fornication? Why is "safe sex" both an immoral position and actually quite "unsafe," given the millions of abortions and unexpected/unwanted pregnancies among the young today?

2. Even if there is no adultery in a marriage, does not every spouse experience envy and jealousy when one or the other acts unsuitably toward a man or woman outside the marriage? How do we help each other overcome the "itch" that threatens to draw us away from each other?

3. In training our children, how do we show them the difference between right and wrong? Are we getting enough help on this from the Catholic school, the pulpit, and the religious education classes? What greater support should we have?

Focus

Fidelity in marriage means much more than abstaining from adultery. All religious ideals are positive, not negative. Husband and wife are pledges of eternal love. Their union in the flesh has a grace which prepares them for union with God. Marital fidelity is not something added to love. It is the very form and expression of that love. It is not a surrender to the domination of a spouse, for love is not a fusion but a communion.

The passing of time wears out bodies, but nothing can make a soul vanish or diminish its eternal value. Nothing on earth is stronger than the fidelity of hearts fortified by the Sacrament of Marriage. They become like the unshakable columns of the Roman Forum against which the ravages of time are powerless. Pleasure happens for a moment. Fidelity is an engagement with the future.

Archbishop Fulton J. Sheen, *Three to Get Married*

Part Three

Commandments: The Faith Lived

Chapter 42

Christian Morality Is Life in Christ

Incorporated into Christ by Baptism, Christians are "dead to sin and alive to God in Christ Jesus . . ." (Rom 6:11).

Catechism, 1694

Luke, in his Acts of the Apostles, considered St. Paul's conversion to Christ so important that he tells the story three times. Paul attributed all his subsequent spiritual growth to his life "in Christ Jesus," a phrase he used dozens of times in his sermons and letters. Jesus was the secret weapon for his moral development.

The third part of the *Catechism* focuses on Christian morality. After the creed as faith professed, and sacraments as faith celebrated, the *Catechism* turns our attention to the faith lived. It deals with this issue in two major sections. The first section establishes the context for Christian morality. The second section analyzes the Ten Commandments. This approach preserves the *Catechism*'s resolute insistence on the primacy of God's initiative through Revelation, salvation, and grace, followed by our human response in faith, celebration, and Christian witness. Hence morality does not begin with the rules but with the call to life in Christ and the Holy Spirit. Covenant love comes first, then the response of Christian affection in the life of the commandments. This saves us both from legalism and from piety without practical witness.

Christian moral teaching begins with a vision of human dignity based on being an image of God. As images of God we are capable of knowing, loving, and serving him, and each other. We discern our call to an eternal destiny, lived on earth by acquiring the happiness attitudes embraced in the eight beatitudes.

We also image God by entering into a community of persons and thus reflecting the loving communion of Father, Son, and Spirit. Our human dignity causes us to experience our God-given freedom as well as the response-ability to covenant with the Lord.

On our moral journey we have the assistance of the *Catechism* for understanding these essential elements: the morality of human acts, 1749-1761; the morality of our passions, 1762-1775; conscience, its judgments, its formation, its choices, 1776-1802.

Central to moral growth is the Spirit-assisted acquisition of virtues. The cardinal virtues of prudence, justice, temperance, and fortitude along with the theological virtues of faith, hope, and charity are the seven good habits of highly effective Christians. Grooved into our minds, wills, and souls, these habits turn us to God and strengthen us to resist evil. These inner powers are essential to Christian character formation (see *Catechism*, 1803-1845.)

To acquire these virtues we are helped by the seven gifts of the Holy Spirit: wisdom, knowledge, understanding, courage, counsel, piety, and fear of the Lord. The harmonious interplay between the gifts and the virtues constitute a powerful source for moral living.

The creed and the sacraments become twin towers of strength for our Christian moral struggle. Faith in God's Revelation of salvation and the experience of that redemption in the sacraments are powerful divine forces making our morality possible.

By beginning with life in Christ and the Spirit, the Church teaches us that Christian morality is impossible without divine help and identity with divine life. We clearly do not walk alone. Nor should we. Jesus and the Spirit walk with us on the moral road to the Father. How blessed we are!

Reflection

1. *What is the foundation for Christian morality?*
   "The first and last point of reference for this catechesis will always be Jesus Christ himself, who is 'the way, and the truth, and the life' (Jn 14:6). . . . 'For to me, to live is Christ' (Phil 1:21)" (*Catechism*, 1698).

2. *How is human dignity related to Christian morality?*
   "The dignity of the human person is rooted in his creation in the image and likeness of God. . . . By his deliberate actions, the human person does, or does not, conform to the good promised by God and attested by moral conscience" (*Catechism*, 1700).

3. *What gift sustains our life of virtue?*
   "The moral life of Christians is sustained by the gifts of the Holy Spirit. These are permanent dispositions which can make man docile in following the promptings of the Holy Spirit" (*Catechism*, 1830).

Prayer

O Jesus, be my way, my truth, my life. Holy Spirit give me the gifts that make my Christian moral life possible.

Resource

Catechism, 1691-1845

Glossary

Cardinal Virtues. These are prudence, justice, temperance, and fortitude. Humility "grounds" the acquisition of these virtues. The seven gifts of the Holy Spirit help us develop the seven theological and cardinal virtues. Together they launch us on a powerful moral life in Jesus and the Spirit.

Theological Virtues. The virtues of faith, hope, and charity that come to us from the graces of the Holy Spirit.

Life Application

1. When I think of the moral life, which of the following terms leap into my mind: vices? commandments? virtues? gifts of the Spirit? beatitudes? Which ones do I never associate with morality? What do my choices say about my moral outlook?

2. When I think of myself as an image of God, what comes to mind? What should I think? Why is an adequate self-understanding as image of God important for moral living? Why not just concentrate on sin and obeying commandments?

3. Read again the chapters on the Holy Spirit. How does the work of the Spirit affect my morality? How critical is the right approach to morality for me and my family?

Focus

Our character, basically, is a composite of our habits. "Sow a thought, reap an action; sow an action, reap a habit; sow a habit, reap a character; sow a character, reap a destiny," the maxim goes.

Habits are powerful factors in our lives. Because they are consistent, often unconscious patterns, they constantly, daily, express our character and produce our effectiveness . . . or ineffectiveness. . . .

Habits, too, have tremendous gravity pull — more than most people realize or would admit. Breaking deeply imbedded habitual tendencies such as procrastination, impatience, criticalness, or selfishness that violate basic principles of human effectiveness involves more than a little willpower and a few minor changes in our lives. "Lift off" takes a tremendous effort, but once we break out of the gravity pull, our freedom takes on a whole new dimension.

Stephen Covey, *The 7 Habits of Highly Effective People*

Chapter 43

What Is a Christian Moral Life?

The Gospel is the revelation in Jesus Christ of God's mercy to sinners.
Catechism, 1846

Jesus is just as interested in saving sinners as many of them are in being saved. He testifies to this in his parables of the lost sheep, the lost coin, and the lost son (Lk 15). But once one is converted, there is still a lifetime of Christian moral living ahead. What does this entail?

1. *The moral life is always a response to God's love.* When Jesus forgave the sins of the woman in the house of Simon the Pharisee, he told the guests, "her many sins have been forgiven; hence, she has shown great love" (Lk 7:47). Covenant love grounds morality.

2. *Resolve to do God's will.* Where is God's will found? In four pillars of fire: the natural law, the revealed commandments, the teachings of Christ, and the direction of a Spirit-guided Church. In our sinful condition there is ambiguity, complexity, and darkness. But the light of God's will shines in this darkness through the four graced pillars of fire. We use these to form our consciences. In addition, the light of our reason (itself a gift of God) has three wonderful revelation-partners in the commandments, the Gospels, and the Magisterium of the Church.

3. *Admit the existence of sin.* Sin abounds here. Think of the Holocaust, ethnic cleansing, pervasive poverty and injustice, cheating, lying, stealing, and abuse of children. Sin is the conscious and deliberate refusal to do God's will. Sin rejects God's friendship. Sin refuses love of God, others, and self. Sin is evil and self-destructive. It abandons moral responsibility. We must *repent* of our sins and have a *lifelong conversion.*

4. *Emphasize the power of grace and the call to holiness.* Sin is obviously powerful. Christ's grace is stronger. "[W]here sin increased, grace overflowed all the more" (Rom 5:20). Be convinced that the positive power of grace will far outweigh the drag of sin. Grace is just as real as sin — and far more powerful.

5. *Practice lifelong moral conversion.* Jesus, John the Baptist, Peter, and Paul insistently call for repentance of sins, moral change, and lifelong conversion. This is one of Revelation's strongest messages. Christian morality is not easy, but we have the love-power of the Holy Spirit to make it possible. In our self-fulfillment culture, Christian morality calls for self-sacrifice. Jesus said that discipleship means: Lose the self. Take the cross. Follow me.

The lives of saints and other outstanding Christians remind us of this. Their moral witness inspires us to have confidence that Christian morality is possible even in the most hostile of cultures. They help us turn away from sin and darkness and put to death our tendencies to pride, lust, selfishness, and hatred. This brings the Paschal mystery into practical terms. We experience that mystery in the sacraments, but we must witness it in our daily lives.

Grace conquers our sin in the Sacrament of Reconciliation. In the reconciliation room, the principles outlined here come together. Divine light shines in the "Peace Room." Empowered by the Spirit, we embark again on our lifelong moral conversion.

Reflection

1. *What is encompassed by the moral law?*

   "The natural law expresses the original moral sense which enables man to discern by reason the good and the evil."

   "The Old Law is the first stage of revealed Law. Its moral prescriptions are summed up in the Ten Commandments."

   "The Old Law is a *preparation for the Gospel*."

   "The New Law or the Law of the Gospel is the perfection here on earth of the divine law, natural and revealed." (*Catechism*, 1954, 1962, 1964, 1965).

2. *What is sin?*

   "Sin is an offense against reason, truth, and right conscience; it is failure in genuine love for God and neighbor. . . . It has been defined as 'an utterance, a deed, or a desire contrary to the eternal law' " (*Catechism*, 1849; see also 1846-1876).

3. *What is grace?*

   "The grace of the Holy Spirit has the power to justify us, that is, to cleanse us from our sins and to communicate to us the 'righteousness of God through faith in Jesus Christ' and through Baptism (Rom 3:22)."

   "Grace is *favor*, the *free and undeserved help* that God gives us to respond to his call to become children of God, adoptive sons, partakers of the divine nature and of eternal life" (*Catechism* 1987, 1996; see also 1987-2005).

Prayer

Come, Holy Spirit! Help us to respond to your call to holiness. Show us how to do the will of God with faith and obedience. Make us honest in admitting the existence of sin, especially our own sins. Motivate us to life-long conversion.

Resource
Catechism, 1846-2051

Glossary
Formation of Conscience. Our conscience should be our moral guide about what's right and wrong. But it needs to be formed throughout our lives by: (1) natural law; (2) the divinely revealed command-ments; (3) the teachings of Christ; (4) the teachings of the Spirit-guided Church (Magisterium).

Mortal Sin. A grave act against the laws of God and a turning away from God. It destroys the life of grace in our souls.

Sin. The breaking of our relationship to God, others, and self. Sin is also a breaking of God's commandments.

Venial Sin. Weakens, but does not destroy, the life of grace in us.

Life Application
1. I know that my conscience is my guide to what is right and wrong. But conscience needs lifelong formation. How much do I turn to the Church, the Gospels, the commandments, and the natural law to form it? How convinced am I that my freedom must be consistent with moral truth?
2. How honest am I about the reality of sin? My sin? What pressures do I experience which cause me to ignore or deny my sinfulness? Why is it spiritually healthier for me to confront sin rather than deny it?
3. How interested am I in the power of grace and the call to holiness? What am I doing about the call? Why do we say that the unexamined life is not worth living?

Focus
The distinctiveness with which the conscience of a child tells him what is right and wrong should be mentioned. As persons advance in life, and yield to temptations which come upon them, they lose this original endowment. They are obliged to grope about by mere reason.

If they debate whether they should act this way or that, and there are many considerations of duty and interest involved in the decision, they feel altogether perplexed. Really and truly not from self deception, but they really do not know how they ought to act. They are obliged to draw out arguments and take a great deal of pains to come to a conclusion. They have lost through sinning a guide which they originally had from God.

But "those who follow the Lamb wherever he goes" have the minds of children. They are able to decide questions of duty at once, undisturbed by the complexity of discordant arguments.

John Henry Cardinal Newman,
Parochial and Plain Sermons

Chapter 44

The First Commandment
— Love God Totally

> The commandments then make explicit the response of love that man is called to give to his God.
>
> *Catechism*, 2083

A father asked his son, "What did you learn in religion class today?" The boy answered, "We studied the Ten Commandments. We learned they are always broke."

A mother wondered if her daughter was learning the Ten Commandments in her religious studies. Her daughter paused and then said, "Oh, I know what you mean now. Yes, we do study the ten suggestions."

Jesus liked to talk about the commandments, but always within the context of the two greatest ones: Love God totally. Love your neighbor as yourself. At Sinai, God reviewed for Israel his liberating works for them. "You see, I love you." Israel accepted from God his love and the Ten Commandments. Keeping them was their way of saying, "We love you too."

Each commandment contains a positive virtue that strengthens our love of God, others, and self. It also expresses a negative restriction against deeds that weaken love.

The first commandment asks us to have a personal relationship with God. This means having living faith in a true God. Our spiritual life begins with faith, hope, and love, powerful virtues that bind us to God. The Holy Spirit provides us with these gifts. They lead to adoration, prayer, and sacrifice — acts that flow freely and spontaneously from our joyful experience of the living God.

A healthy relationship with God liberates us from superstition, a magic mentality, and idolatry. We are able to resist the temptation to make a god out of sex, money, or power. God frees us from reducing him to a super parent, a policeman, or a justification for our own prejudices. A loving union with God helps us keep our faith in balance while coping with the forces of secularism in our contemporary society. Our total love of God saves us from the dead ends of atheism and agnosticism. The atheist denies God's existence. The agnostic claims nothing can be known about God. Many reasons account for these aberrations. Sometimes it is the failure of faith witness on the part of believers that causes loss of belief by others.

We respond to this by our faith in God, which is the best way to affirm human dignity, since God created us and knows how to bring us to fulfillment. We affirm our hope in the future life, which motivates us more powerfully to carry out our duties here on earth.

Our faith in God should cause a commitment to justice for the oppressed and economic fairness for all. We witness to our unbelieving brothers and sisters how our faith helps us deal with the problems of life and death, guilt, and suffering — difficulties which often drive them to despair.

Our love for God teaches us that God's commandments are in harmony with the most secret desires of our hearts. God is giving us life, light, hope, and freedom. Without God there will be death, darkness, despair, and bondage. We should reach out to unbelievers with this medicine of mercy and hope.

It is no coincidence that the first article of the creed ("I believe in God") and the first commandment contain the same religious call. Religion begins with God, whether in a faith statement or a moral outcome. Happily, the grace of the Spirit makes this possible. Come again and again, O Holy Spirit.

Reflection

1. *What does the first commandment ask of us?*
   " 'You shall love the Lord your God with all your heart, and with all your soul and with all your strength' (Deut 6:5).
   "The first commandment summons man to believe in God, to hope in him, and to love him above all else" (*Catechism*, 2133-2134).

2. *How does our religion fulfill this commandment?*
   "Adoring God, praying to him, offering him the worship that belongs to him, fulfilling the promises and vows made to him are acts of the virtue of religion which fall under obedience to the first commandment" (*Catechism*, 2135).

3. *From what acts does this commandment liberate us?*
   We are liberated from superstition, a magic mentality, idolatry, irreligion, atheism, and agnosticism (see *Catechism*, 2110-2128 and 2138-2140).

Prayer

"How I love your law, O LORD / It is my meditation all the day. / Your command has made me wiser than my enemies, / . . . Through your precepts I gain discernment; / . . . A lamp to my feet is your word, / . . . Your decrees are my inheritance forever."

Ps 119:97-8, 104-5, 111

Resource
Catechism, 2083-2141

Glossary
Agnosticism. Claims one cannot know whether God exists or not.
Atheism. Denial of God's existence.
Secularist. Appears not to care about God's existence.

Life Application
1. What link can I see between the first commandment and the beginning of the Apostles' Creed? What are five signs in my life that affirm my faith in God? How does my idea of God differ from when I was a child?
2. What kind of a case for God's existence would I make to an atheist, agnostic, or secularist? It has been said, "Win an argument and lose a soul." How would that affect my witnessing of my faith?
3. What stories can I share about people I know who have come to faith in God? Why must I connect a life of love and justice with my faith in God? What are some false gods people worship today?

Focus
Faith in God presupposes an awareness of the presence of God. It involves not only an attitude to the holy but also a way of relating oneself [to everyday life].

God's temple is a sanctuary without walls. If the sanctuary is everywhere, then we can sense the ark or the altar somewhere. . . .

Religion in America is inclined to follow rather than to challenge the general trends of opinion, as if the task of religion were to serve as a handmaid of civilization. . . .

The Bible may be found in hotels, but it is not to be found in the homes or in the minds. Only few of our contemporaries have ever absorbed the challenge of the prophets or the grandeur of the book of Genesis, though they have attended Sunday school and were thrilled with the confirmation ceremonies. What prevails in the field of religion is intellectual as well as spiritual illiteracy, ignorance as well as idolatry of false values. We have a generation devoid of learning as well as of sensitivity. . . .

. . . If the divine likeness is our premise, then the question arises, How should a being created in the likeness of God act, think, feel?

Abraham Joshua Heschel

Chapter 45

The Second Commandment — Reverence the Sacred

> Preaching and catechizing should be permeated with adoration and respect for the name of our Lord Jesus Christ.
>
> *Catechism*, 2145

In an article, "Which Mountain Did Moses Climb?" Gordon Gaskill described his pilgrimage to Mount Sinai. On the morning of the climb, he heard the bells of St. Catherine's monastery pealing thirty-three times, one for each year of Jesus' life. Jewish hikers crawled out of their sleeping bags. Christians made coffee. The Moslem guide touched his head to the ground for the first prayer of the day. Gaskill said the experience was "out of this world."

That sense of the sacred is the message of the second commandment. We are invited to be aware of God's sacred presence in the midst of life. Our experience of God's holiness generates a reverence for God, for people, and for nature.

When Moses approached the burning bush, he heard God tell him to take off his shoes, for he stood on holy ground (Ex 3:1-7). He felt contradictory emotions. Fascination drew him to the strange fire. Awe restrained him. God's attractiveness pulled him forward. God's majesty gave him pause and sent him to his knees.

God was teaching Moses reverence. Moses could see the sacred in the midst of life. He learned he must not trivialize or reduce the sacred to just another thrill. God's name, which reveals his person, deserves respect.

The second commandment stresses reverence for God's name. Old Testament people took this so seriously that they never spoke God's name, but used synonyms. Only the High Priest could pronounce the holy name at special Temple liturgies.

Our reverence for God and his holy name means we should never make wrong use of the divine name. This would happen in blasphemy and perjury in God's name. Wrong use of God's power is at stake here. People have used God's name to justify wars, the slaughter of enemies, and the imposition of tyranny on others. Tragically, some have invoked the God of love to support hatred, the God of trust to enhance betrayal, and the God of mercy to justify the unwillingness to forgive.

Misuse of God's name tries to drive the sacred out of the world. It causes us to say, "Is there nothing sacred any more?" It engenders sacrilege, which debases holy places and even the Blessed Sacrament itself. But once we banish the sacred and the attitude of reverence which responds to it, then we are all at risk. Respect for God grounds respect for life. Desecrate (i.e. *de-sacralize*) God and then we will desecrate one another. Destroy the holy Name and then do not be surprised that all else is fair game. The best way to banish savagery is to honor the sacred.

Popular music, films, TV shows, and novels are filled with irreverent use of the name of Jesus Christ in an ambience of vulgar talk. Children, parents, teachers, employers, and employees curse one another. Not only is a linguistic truce and cleansing needed, but a positive recovery of self-respect based on a reverence for God.

God does not want us to practice self-denigration in a cross fire of wounding expletives. God honors each of us with infinite care. When we treat God the way he treats us, then we will begin to respect each other.

Reflection

1. *What is the call of the second commandment?*

    "You shall not take the name of the Lord your God in vain" (Deut 5:11).

    "The second commandment enjoins respect for the Lord's name."

    "Respect for his name is an expression of the respect owed to the mystery of God himself and to the whole sacred reality it evokes. The *sense of the sacred* is part of the virtue of religion . . ." (*Catechism*, 2161, 2144).

2. *What are some things this commandment forbids?*

    It forbids the abuse of God's name and that of Jesus Christ. It opposes blasphemy, false oaths (perjury) taken in God's name and sacrilege (cf. *Catechism*, 2162-2163; see also 2120).

3. *Why are our names holy?*

    "God calls each one by name. Everyone's name is sacred. The name is the icon of the person. It demands respect as a sign of the dignity of the one who bears it" (*Catechism*, 2158).

Prayer

"Lord, our Lord, / how glorious is your name over all the earth."

Ps 8:1

Resource

Catechism, 2142-2166

Glossary

Awe and Wonder. Attitudes that draw us to God and cause us to reverence his holiness. We accept intimacy with God but never forget that God is "other" than ourselves.

Blasphemy. A wrong use of God's name, a disrespectful approach to God, a disdain for God, and a rejection of the love God offers to us.

The Sacred. Also the holy, refers to the absolute love, purity, and beauty of God. It is a characteristic of the mystery, uniqueness, and integrity of God.

Life Application

1. What do I think is the cause of the growth of vulgar language even in children, heard in schools, playgrounds, and even at home? What do I think when I hear Jesus' name thrown around in films as an expletive, a careless and offensive use of his holy name? What should be done to restore discipline in language?

2. When "nothing is sacred anymore" can I hope to have people respect each other? There is much talk about self-esteem these days. What is the link between a declining self-esteem and the loss of reverence for God and human persons?

3. If I were to give a family a ten-point plan for the restoration of respect for God, clean language, and the recovery of the sacred in everyday life, what would I suggest?

Focus

Talking to God: in America, as the prophet Amos put it, those conversations flow like a mighty river. This week, if you believe at all in opinion surveys, more of us will pray than will go to work, or exercise, or have sexual relations. . . .

Some of these prayers are born *in extremis*: there are few atheists in cancer wards or unemployment lines. But in allegedly rootless, materialistic, self-centered America, there is also a hunger for a personal experience of God that prayer seeks to satisfy. [Father Andrew] Greeley's studies show that serious prayer usually begins after the age of 30, when the illusion that we are masters of our own fate fades and adults develop a deeper need to call on the Master of the Universe. In an age of relativism, God remains for many the one true absolute. In an era of transience and divorce, God can be the only place left to turn to for unconditioned love.

From "Talking to God," *Newsweek*, January 6, 1992

Chapter 46

The Third Commandment
– The Joy of Worship

The Sunday celebration of the Lord's Day and his Eucharist is at the heart of the Church's life.

Catechism, 2177

The happy hedonist says, "I work six days. I save the seventh for recreation. Church can't compete with boating, cycling, mountain climbing, skiing, aerobic dancing. When it comes to priorities, I come first. If I can't be happy, there is no way I can make others happy."

This hedonist has a partial insight into the full meaning of the biblical sabbath. The sabbath is indeed meant to be a day for resting from our labors. The hedonist's error is ignoring the other purpose of the sabbath, which is to worship and thank God for the gifts of the earth which he is obviously enjoying so much. Gratitude is the memory of the heart. The hedonist takes the gift, but fails to acknowledge the giver. All he has left is graceless self-indulgence.

The sabbath remembers creation. God "worked" six days and rested on the seventh. The prophets taught that the sabbath was also a day to remember God's gifts to Israel, above all the liberation from slavery in Egypt and the covenant at Sinai. The sabbath was a day to rest and renew one's humanity. It was also a day to praise and thank God for the gifts of creation and salvation.

The Christian Sunday contains both of these elements of the biblical sabbath – rest and adoration. Because Jesus rose from the dead on a Sunday, Christianity moved the sabbath from Saturday to Sunday. As the first day of the week, Sunday symbolizes the beginning of the new creation in Christ.

The Christian Sunday fulfills the meaning of the Jewish sabbath in the Paschal mystery of Christ. It proclaims the eternal rest of man with God. Sunday Eucharist observes a moral prescription naturally inscribed in the heart of man. St. Thomas says we should render to God public, visible, and regular worship which recognizes God's universal good will toward us.

On Sundays (or Saturday evenings) and other holy days of obligation, Catholics are bound to participate in the Mass. "Those who deliberately fail in this obligation commit a grave sin" (*Catechism*, 2181). Communal celebration of the Eucharist is a witness to Christ's fidelity to his Church. The faithful, by their participation in the Mass, joyfully witness the holiness of God and their hope for salvation.

Sunday should ideally be a day of rest, relaxation, family renewal, and the sanctity of the family meal. True, the complexity of modern society means that many will have to work on Sunday. In this case, people should set aside their "day off" for this purpose. We all need "letting-go time" for personal refreshment, meditation, silence, perspective, and prayer.

Keeping holy the sabbath is an invitation to become re-created. This is done by participation in the creative force of the Eucharistic celebration and by spiritual, emotional, and physical renewal. Sunday is a divinely appointed renewal day through worship, exercise, relaxation, and reflection. It creates the climate for conversion and personal growth. Keeping the sabbath is a commitment to wholeness — human and divine.

Reflection

1. *What is the lesson of the third commandment?*

   " 'Observe the sabbath day, to keep it holy' (Deut 5:12). . . .

   "The sabbath, which represented the completion of the first creation, has been replaced by Sunday which recalls the new creation inaugurated by the Resurrection of Christ" (*Catechism*, 2189-2190).

2. *What does Sunday observance include?*

   " 'On Sundays and other holy days of obligation the faithful are bound to participate in the Mass.'

   " '[They should also] abstain from those labors and business concerns which impede the worship to be rendered to God, the joy which is proper to the Lord's Day, or the proper relaxation of mind and body' (Codex Iuris Canonici, can. 1247)" (*Catechism*, 2192-2193).

3. *Why does Sunday call for rest?*

   "The institution of Sunday helps all 'to be allowed sufficient rest and leisure to cultivate their familial, cultural, social, and religious lives' " (*Catechism*, 2194).

Prayer

Lord, teach us to observe the Christian Sunday by participation in Eucharist and personal and familial renewal.

Resource

Catechism, 2168-2195

Glossary

Christian Sunday. Carries forward the biblical meaning of sabbath. Relaxation should be accompanied by participation in the celebration of the Eucharist to praise and thank God for the gift of salvation and the benefits of creation.

Holy Days of Obligation. Special days on which Catholics are required to go to Mass. These are Christmas, Immaculate Conception, All Saints, Assumption, Ascension, and the Solemnity of the Mother of God.

Sabbath. The biblical seventh day on which God's people were expected to rest from their labors and praise God for the gifts of creation.

Life Application

1. As contemporary culture becomes busier and more fast-paced, does not the wisdom of Sunday rest begin to make more sense? What could my family do to make Sunday more of a family day, with a family meal and some spiritual reflection?

2. Gratitude is the memory of the heart. All we own we owe. How could these truths help me to remain faithful to my Sunday obligation to worship God at Eucharist? If I like to be thanked and appreciated for what I do for others, should I not do the same to God? What other motives help me regarding attendance at Sunday Eucharist?

3. Some say "I want to get something out of Mass." What would happen if they said, "I want to put my whole self into Mass. I want to give God everything I am and have"?

Focus

The Church . . . earnestly desires that Christ's faithful, when present at the Eucharistic mystery of faith, should not be there as strangers or silent spectators. On the contrary, through a good understanding of the rites and prayers they should participate knowingly, devoutly and actively. . . . [B]y offering the Immaculate Victim, not only through the hands of the priest, but also with him, they should learn to offer themselves too. Through Christ the Mediator, they should be drawn day by day into ever closer union with God and each other, so that finally God may be all in all.

Sacrosanctum Concilium, 48; SVC

Chapter 47

The Fourth Commandment
— Empower the Family

The Christian family constitutes . . . a domestic church.

Catechism, 2204

Catholic teaching makes family life a priority. A Synod of Bishops in Rome in 1980 drew up a "Bill of Rights" for families. Some of these rights are:
- the right to have a family and adequate means to support it.
- the right to bring up children in accordance with the family's own traditions and religious and cultural values.
- the right to housing suitable for proper family life.
- the right to protect minors by adequate institutions and laws to fulfill the family's role expeditiously.
- the right to a wholesome recreation that fosters family values (see *Christian Family*, 46).

The fourth commandment fosters family values. A strong family leads to a healthy society and vigorous nation. When the family perceives itself as a "domestic church" where faith, prayer, and love bind the members, then the local and universal Church prospers.

The Christian family should be a communion of persons reflecting the blessed Trinity's inner life of love. Its procreative and educative role mirrors the work of our heavenly Father. The family is called to share in the sacrifice of the Son. The stream of love among the members witnesses the Holy Spirit. This is God's fundamental plan for family life and the basis for authority, obedience, and mutual care among the members.

The honoring of father and mother means that children should respect and obey their parents, and that adults should care for their elderly parents. Filial love is required by divine law. "With your whole heart honor your father; your mother's birthpangs forget not. Remember, of these parents you were born; what can you give them for all they gave you?" (Sir 7:27-28).

Adults should look out for their parents, giving them moral and material support in their old age as far as possible. When elderly parents face loneliness, sickness, and possible destitution, they look to their adult children for support. Covenant love, the basis of family life, requires this.

Christian parents will respect their children as gifts from God and unique persons in their own right. Good parents will provide for the spiritual, material, emotional, educational, and physical needs of their children. As the children develop into adolescence and young adulthood, wise parents will help them toward autonomy and independence.

Children should learn the virtues and habits of prayer, obedience, respect, responsibility, honesty, hard work, willingness to share, and concern for the family. Children should honor, love, and obey their parents and work for the common good of the family.

A Christian home should be a center of forgiveness, respect, rights and obligations, fidelity, and unselfish service for one another. Brothers and sisters should work at harmonious relationships with each other. A spirit of prayer, faith, worship, conscience formation, and a loving consciousness of God is the essential backbone of these family values.

The family is the school of the virtues that trains the members to create an orderly and productive society and nation. In turn, the government should do all it can to make strong family life possible. Similarly, bishops and pastors ought to make the nourishing of strong Catholic families the highest priority. A rich partnership of home, Church, society, and nation is a formula for stability, continuity, and joy.

Reflection

1. *What is the message of the fourth commandment?*
   " 'Honor your father and mother' (Deut 5:16; Mk 7:10)."

   "Children owe their parents respect, gratitude, just obedience, and assistance. . . .

   "Parents have the first responsibility for the education of the children in faith, prayer, and all the virtues. They have the duty to provide as far as possible for the physical and spiritual needs of their children" (*Catechism*, 2247, 2251-2252).

2. *How should parents handle their children's vocation?*
   "Parents should respect and encourage their children's vocations. They should remember and teach that the first calling of the Christian is to follow Jesus" (*Catechism*, 2253).

3. *What are the responsibilities of citizens and nations?*
   "Public authority is obliged to respect the fundamental rights of the human person and the conditions for the exercise of his freedom.

   "It is the duty of citizens to work with civil authority for building up society in a spirit of truth, justice, solidarity, and freedom.

   "Citizens are obliged in conscience not to follow the directives of civil authorities when they are contrary to the demands of the moral order" (*Catechism*, 2254-2256).

Prayer

Lord, bless and strengthen our families and our country. May the example of the Holy Family inspire all Christian families to develop the balance of rights, duties, and responsibilities that bring them strength, cohesiveness, and joy. Create a bond between home, church, school, and government which results in harmony and health for all concerned.

Resource

Catechism, 2197-2256

Glossary

Bill of Rights for Families. A list of rights for support of the family published by the Synod of Bishops in 1980. It dramatizes the highest priority the Church gives to protecting and defending the family.

Communion of Persons. The Trinity is the supreme model of the Communion of persons where absolute unity and love exist. The family should also be such a community striving for the highest ideals of love among the members.

Life Application

1. If and when my parents meet with illness or some form of incapacity, what will I do to help them?
2. How well do I listen to my children's decisions and support them as well as I can in the light of our Catholic faith and morality?
3. How do we — parents, children, siblings — honor and respect each other in our family? How could we improve?

Focus

So blest are they who round a family board
May gather: — May they humbly thank the Lord,
Not only for the food they common share,
But for the dear loved faces circled there:
So oft, unless we face that board alone,
We treasure not its true sweet sense of home.

Donna R. Lydston in *Poems That Touch the Heart*

Chapter 48

The Fifth Commandment – Stop the Killing

God alone is the Lord of life from its beginning until its end.

Catechism, 2258

Victorian British gentlemen, veterans of Queen Victoria's "little wars," were fond of greeting one another with the words "Did you have a good war?" Benjamin Franklin, that most artful of diplomats, would have shaken his head and told them, "There has never been a good war or a bad peace."

After the fall of Adam and Eve, the very first act recorded in Scripture is Cain's murder of Abel. The destruction of human life is the first result of original sin. God condemned the act. "[Y]our brother's blood cries out to me from the soil" (Gn 4:10). God opposes the deliberate and malicious killing of human life. "You shall not kill" (Deut 5:17).

At the same time legitimate self-defense is permitted, both to save one's life and to preserve the common good of the community. The *Catechism* outlines the principles for the defense of one's own life in paragraphs 2263-2267. It sets out the principles for peace and war and the strict guidelines for "legitimate defense by military force" in paragraphs 2302-2317. The emphasis, however, is on the aggressive pursuit of peace and the ways to avoid war. Matters that lead to war should be eliminated: hatred, anger, revenge, massive buildup of armies, economies based on weapons production.

Other deeds opposed by this commandment are: suicide, abortion, euthanasia, infanticide, terrorism, genocide, assassination.

In the case of suicide, the *Catechism* says, "Suicide . . . is gravely contrary to the just love of self . . . neighbor . . . God. . . . Voluntary cooperation with a suicide is against the moral law. Grave psychological disturbances, anguish, or grave fear of hardship, suffering, or torture can diminish the responsibility of the one committing suicide" (2281-2282).

The *Catechism* has a powerful section about the immorality of abortion (see 2270-2275). "The inalienable right to life of every innocent human individual is a constitutive element of a civil society and its legislation" (2273). From the very beginning of Christian history, abortion was forbidden. "You shall not kill the embryo by abortion" (*Didache* [*Doctrine of the Twelve Apostles*], 2, 2 – c. A.D. 60).

The *Catechism* is also very clear about the immorality of euthanasia.

"Those whose lives are diminished or weakened deserve special respect. Sick or handicapped persons should be helped to lead lives as normal as possible. Whatever its motives and means, direct euthanasia consists in putting an end to the lives of handicapped, sick, or dying persons. It is morally unacceptable" (2276-2277). At the same time, the *Catechism* repeats the traditional teaching of the Church that one need not use extraordinary means to stay — or keep someone — alive.

Regarding capital punishment, Pope John Paul II teaches that its use should be very rare: "Today, in fact, as a consequence of the possibilities which the state has for effectively preventing crime, by rendering one who has committed an offense incapable of doing harm — without definitively taking away from him the possibility of redeeming himself — the cases in which the execution of the offender is an absolute necessity 'are very rare, if not practically non-existent' (*Evangelium Vitae*, 56)" (*Catechism*, 2267).

In these many life-and-death issues, the Church has been a clear voice on behalf of life. In a century that has seen the worst wars in history, death camps, legal promotion of abortion (and now, euthanasia), the courageous stand of the Church on the side of life is a sign of hope for human dignity and a summons to societies to wake up their moral consciences.

Reflection

1. *What is the Church's teaching about killing?*
   "You shall not kill" (Deut 5:17).
   "Every human life, from the moment of conception until death, is sacred because the human person has been willed for its own sake in the image and likeness of the living and holy God" (*Catechism*, 2319).

2. *What are some sins forbidden by the fifth commandment?*
   Murder, direct and intended abortion, euthanasia, suicide (see *Catechism*, 2320, 2322, 2324, 2325).

3. *What does the Church say about war?*
   "Legitimate defense can be not only a right but a grave duty for one who is responsible for the lives of others. The defense of the common good requires that an unjust aggressor be rendered unable to cause harm. For this reason, those who legitimately hold authority also have the right to use arms to repel aggressors against the civil community entrusted to their responsibility."
   "Because of the evils and injustices that all war brings with it, we must do everything reasonably possible to avoid it."
   "The Church and human reason assert the permanent validity of the moral law during armed conflicts. Practices deliberately contrary to the

law of nations and to its universal principles are crimes" (*Catechism*, 2265, 2327, 2328).

Prayer
From famine, plague, and war, deliver us, O Lord. From abortion, murder, euthanasia, and suicide, deliver us, O Lord.

Resource
Catechism, 2258-2330

Glossary
Abortion. The killing of a human life still in the womb. We should strive to protect human life from womb to tomb.

Euthanasia. Directly terminating the life of a sick, dying, or handicapped person. It is morally unacceptable.

Suicide. The taking of one's own life. Psychological problems and anxieties resulting from torture can diminish the responsibility of the person. Cooperation in someone's suicide is evil.

Life Application
1. How clear am I about the reasons why abortion is a grave sin? If I were counseling a Catholic who is pro-choice, what would I say? What do I think of Catholic politicians who say that privately they are against abortion but as lawmakers they support it?
2. What is my thinking on capital punishment? Does it deter murder? How ready am I to write a living will or sign a power of attorney concerning "no extraordinary means" to keep me alive in case of terminal illness? Do I understand the Church's opposition to euthanasia? What should I know?
3. What are the many steps my country and each citizen should take to avoid war? Can I justify nuclear war? What would I do if I thought my country initiated an unjust war? What are five compelling reasons for preserving human life?

Focus
Disregard for the sacred character of life in the womb weakens the very fabric of civilization; it prepares a mentality that can lead to the acceptance of other practices against the fundamental rights of the individual. This mentality can . . . undermine concern for those in want, manifesting itself in insensitivity to social needs; it can produce contempt for the elderly,

to the point of advocating euthanasia; it can prepare the way for those forms of genetic engineering that go against life, the dangers of which are not yet fully known to the general public.

It is therefore very encouraging to see [you bishops, here in the United States] constantly holding up to your people the value of human life.

It is also a source of worldwide honor that, in your country, so many upright men and women of differing religious convictions are united in a profound respect for the laws of the Creator and Lord of life. . . .

Pope John Paul II in John Paul II in America

Chapter 49

The Sixth Commandment
– Practice Fidelity

> The union of man and woman in marriage is a way of imitating in the flesh the Creator's generosity and fecundity.
>
> *Catechism*, 2335

In the film *Indecent Proposal*, a rich bachelor offers a married woman a million dollars if she will spend one night with him. In her discussion about it with her husband, she says, "Well, it's only my body, not my mind or emotions." She accepts the proposal with her husband's approval. The rest of the story shows how the adultery nearly wrecks the marriage. The story shows that a complete person was involved, not just a body.

The *Catechism* agrees. "*Sexuality* affects all aspects of the human person in the unity of his body and soul. It especially concerns affectivity, the capacity to love and to procreate, and in a more general way the aptitude for forming bonds of communion with others" (2332).

The *Catechism* treats of chastity, and the sins against it, in sections 2337-2359. But we will treat chastity in our chapter on the ninth commandment, thus combining the *Catechism*'s coverage of chastity in both the sixth and ninth commandments.

The other major issue addressed by this commandment is marriage. Pope John Paul II has frequently spoken and written on the subject of marriage, and never so eloquently as he did in his 1979-80 Wednesday sermons on the creation stories in Genesis (read *Original Unity of Man and Woman*, Boston: Daughters of St. Paul, 1981).

Following the teaching of Jesus, who pointed his listeners back to the steps in the creation and marriage of Adam and Eve, the Pope develops a theology of marriage that flows from husband and wife as images of God. The spouses image God as a communion of persons (the Trinity) by becoming a communion of persons themselves. They image God's absolute faithfulness to his covenant with us, by fidelity to their covenant with each other.

The bond between husband and wife is both procreative and conjugal. The aspect of conjugal, mutual love is called "unitive." The aspect of the "procreative" concerns the conception, birth, and education of children. The bond between the conjugal and procreative may not be broken (*see Catechism*, 2369). Read again our treatment of this same subject in our chapter 40, on the Sacrament of Matrimony.

The *Catechism* addresses the issues of artificial contraception (not approved) and the regulation of births (approved with set conditions) in paragraphs 2366-2372.

Sexuality is seen as a positive force, integral to the spouses, symbolizing and reinforcing both the conjugal and procreative aspects of marriage. Sex is only permissible within marriage.

Sins against marriage are adultery, divorce, incest, polygamy, and "free love." Jesus condemned adultery of the body and the heart (lust) (see Mt 5:32; 19:6). Jesus taught that marriage should be indissoluble (see Mt 5:31-32; 19:3-9). The Church's teaching on divorce is found in paragraphs 2382-2386.

The *Catechism*'s discussion of marriage stresses God's loving intentions for marriage, the ideals of love, covenant and responsibility, the procreation of children, the positive contribution of sexuality to both love and procreation, the good of society, and the sources of happiness.

While homosexual acts are contrary to the intent of the sixth commandment and natural law, the *Catechism* notes: "The number of men and women who have deep-seated homosexual tendencies is not negligible. This inclination, which is objectively disordered, constitutes for most of them a trial. They must be accepted with respect, compassion, and sensitivity. Every sign of unjust discrimination in their regard should be avoided. These persons are called to fulfill God's will in their lives and, if they are Christians, to unite to the sacrifice of the Lord's Cross the difficulties they may encounter from their condition" (*Catechism*, 2358).

Reflection

1. *What is the teaching of the sixth commandment?*
   "You shall not commit adultery" (Deut 5:18).
   "The covenant which spouses have freely entered into entails faithful love. It imposes on them the obligation to keep their marriage indissoluble" (*Catechism*, 2397).

2. *What about procreation?*
   "Fecundity is a good, a gift and an end of marriage. By giving life, spouses participate in God's fatherhood" (*Catechism*, 2398).

3. *What is to be said about the regulation of birth?*
   "The regulation of births represents one of the aspects of responsible fatherhood and motherhood. Legitimate intentions on the part of the spouses do not justify recourse to morally unacceptable means (for example, direct sterilization or contraception)" (*Catechism*, 2399).

Prayer

Lord, bless the love, fruitfulness, and fidelity of married couples. Impart to them the wisdom to live according to the divine plan and to strengthen family values by every possible means.

Resource

Catechism, 2331-2400

Glossary

Artificial Contraception. The use of a pill or other device to prevent conception in the marital act.

Adultery. Sex outside of marriage involving a married person.

Fornication. Sex outside of marriage between two unmarried people.

Incest. Sex between a parent and a son or daughter, or between other close relatives.

Natural Family Planning. A permissible regulation of births with certain conditions (see *Catechism*, 2366-2372).

Life Application

1. How does sexuality affect my body and my emotions? How can sexuality be an expression of, and a help to, love between spouses?
2. Why is fidelity so essential to marriage? What must I do to be faithful to God's laws about sexual expression?
3. What are the unitive and procreative aspects of marriage? Why must the bond between the unitive and procreative never be broken?

Focus

Father, by your plan man and woman are united and married life has been established as the one blessing that was not forfeited by original sin or washed away in the flood. Look with love upon this woman, your daughter, now joined to her husband in marriage. Give her the grace of love and peace. May she always follow the example of the holy women whose praises are sung in the Scriptures.

May her husband put his trust in her and recognize that she is his equal and the heir with him in the life of grace. May he always honor her and love her as Christ loves his bride, the Church.

The Church takes part in your joy and with an open heart receives you, together with your parents and friends, on the day in which before God our Father you establish between yourselves a partnership for the whole of your lives.

Nuptial Blessing "A," *Sacramentary*

Chapter 50

The Seventh Commandment
– Be Honest and Just

Christian life strives to order this world's goods to God and to fraternal charity.

Catechism, 2401

In biblical society, most people owned little. They had no savings, no state-supported safety net against starvation, homelessness, or sickness. A robber who stole a winter robe exposed the victim to freezing. A predator who stole sheep from a shepherd in a hand-to-mouth economy could ruin a family. When rich people did these things to the poor, prophets cried to heaven for justice.

Survival societies know best the wisdom of the seventh commandment. Survival groups in rich societies know well its call for mercy and justice. Stealing harms the individual and the society. It deprives the poor of the little they have and erodes trust, which is the glue of the social order.

The *Catechism* outlines the moral principles implied by the seventh commandment. God willed that the goods of the earth be used for the common good of all. We have a right to private property, but it should benefit others as well as oneself. In economic matters, human dignity demands the practice of the virtue of temperance to moderate attachment to worldly goods. It also calls for justice that protects people's rights, and it urges solidarity with the poor. Hence we should not steal from another, cheat in business, pay unfair salaries, or exploit others' weaknesses or distress to make money. Promises and contracts should be made and kept in good faith and with fairness.

The *Catechism* broadly outlines the fundamentals of the social teaching of the Church in paragraphs 2419-2449. See also *Catechism* 1877-1948, where it deals with the person and society, the common good, and social justice. Christian revelation calls for a deeper understanding of the laws of the social order. The Church exercises a moral judgment on economic and social issues when the fundamental rights of the person and the salvation of souls are at stake. The social teaching of the Church proposes principles for reflection, criteria for judgment, and directions for action.

The rise of the modern industrial society prompted the Church to make fresh applications of the Gospel to the social order. Popes from Leo XIII to the present day have developed this social teaching. Pope John XXIII taught that peace will come more easily when people are treated justly. Pope Paul VI argued that the rich nations of the world have a responsibility to help the poor ones. Pope John Paul II has said the state has an essential obligation to assure that workers can enjoy the fruits of their labor. While the state has an obligation to protect human rights in the economic sector, the primary responsibility for this belongs to the institutions, groups, and associations that make up a society.

The *Catechism* concludes this section with an exhortation to love the poor. It cites the corporal and spiritual works of mercy and many biblical passages that deal with concern for the poor. "Love for the poor is incompatible with immoderate love of riches or their selfish use" (2445). St. Rose of Lima carries the point as well as anyone: "When we serve the poor and the sick, we serve Jesus. We must not neglect to help our neighbor, because it is Jesus whom we serve."

Reflection

1. *What is the message of the seventh commandment?*
   "You shall not steal" (Deut 5:19).
      "The seventh commandment enjoins the practice of justice and charity in the administration of earthly goods and the fruits of men's labor" (*Catechism*, 2451).

2. *What is an essential feature of the Church's social teaching?*
   "The Church makes a judgment about economic and social matters when the fundamental rights of the person or the salvation of souls requires it. She is concerned with the temporal common good of men because they are ordered to the sovereign Good, their ultimate end" (*Catechism*, 2458).

3. *For whom is social and economic life?*
   "Man is himself the author, center, and goal of all economic and social life. The decisive point of the social question is that goods created by God for everyone should in fact reach everyone in accordance with justice and with the help of charity" (*Catechism*, 2459).

Prayer

O Lord, hear the cry of the poor and help us to hear and respond to that cry with a generous, loving, and just heart. May we serve others as serving Jesus himself.

Resource
Catechism, 2401-2463

Glossary
Social Teachings of the Church. Refers specifically to papal teachings about social morality applied to a world where the industrial and technological revolutions raise issues about wealth, poverty, and human dignity. Beginning with Pope Leo XIII's *Rerum Novarum* to the present, these teachings form a body of developing guidance on the social order.

Life Application
1. When the U.S. bishops wrote a pastoral letter about peace and the immorality of nuclear war, many praised it. When they wrote about the economy and the needs of the poor, many said they should stay with religious topics and mind their own business. What do I think about this?
2. How aware am I that the Church has a social teaching? What do I know about it? Isn't the seventh commandment more about shoplifting, tax evasion, convenience store hold-ups, etc., than about justice for the poor, elderly, and homeless and the grief that the greed of big business causes in society? (Explain your reaction.)
3. If my house has been burglarized or I have been mugged, what has that to do with the seventh commandment? What are the virtues people should acquire to avoid stealing?

Focus
Trusting societies always have a sense of the divine presence. In ethnic neighborhoods people nourished their souls in parish churches. In small towns they drew a feeling for God and the power to trust and be honest from the churches on the commons. The hymns that rang from open windows on Sunday morning consecrated the land and the people therein. The people professed their faith in a God who lovingly trusted them and showed them what it felt like. Contact with the spiritual made their neighborhoods and towns centers of trust and honesty.

That spiritual power is still present and available in our mega-cities and apartment/condo towers. The leaders of all religions are aware of their responsibility to nourish community and fix a new glue for fresh forms of gathering in a disparate society. New networks are arising for safe neighborhoods and a trusting, cooperative human family. This is the positive vision of the seventh commandment.

Chapter 51

The Eighth Commandment – Tell the Truth

The disciple of Christ consents to "live in the truth". . . .

Catechism, 2470

In Shakespeare's *Hamlet* when young Laertes is about to leave home and embark on his career, he asks his father, Polonius, for guidance. His dad delivers a series of proverbs about right living. Finally, he says, "This above all, to thine own self be true, / And it must follow, as the night the day, / Thou canst not then be false to any man." In other words, "Be an honest man, my son." Polonius knew the value of truthful living.

We rightly associate Jesus with love. We should also link him with truth. Christ's message of love was effective because it was true. Jesus claimed he not only preached truth but also said, "I am . . . the truth" (Jn 14:6). Jesus lived truth. He told Pilate, "I came into the world . . . to testify to the truth" (Jn 18:37).

Pilate had spent his professional life with liars, flatterers, and political expedience. He was deaf to truth: "What is truth?" (Jn 18:38). This skeptical question endures today. Relativism prevails today. It preaches that one cannot know truth, only opinions. But when there is a lack of confidence that truth exists and can be known, then lying becomes a way of life.

But we instinctively hunger for truth. Rightly, we want others to say what they mean and mean what they say. We want truth in advertising and credibility from public leaders in all walks of life. Spouses, parents, and children expect truth telling and truthful living from each other. How else can trust grow?

The best way to evaluate the truth-telling in another is to watch his behavior. Witness is the key. The *Catechism* says the martyr (means "witness") is "the supreme witness . . . to the truth of the faith" (2473). When someone dies to defend the truth of the Gospel, that is the most powerful argument on behalf of Gospel truth.

Sins against this commandment include slander, perjury, false witness, ruining another's reputation, all forms of deceit and lies – whether spoken at a personal level or by public leaders and their communications offices. The *Catechism* devotes a special section on the truth-telling responsibilities of the media and all agencies that use the powerful means of modern communications (2493-2499).

"It is necessary that all members of society meet the demands of justice and charity in this domain. They should help, through the means of social communications, in the formation and diffusion of sound public opinion" (2495).

The *Catechism* also devotes a section to truth and its relation to beauty and art (2500-2503). ". . . of their nature [the arts] are directed toward expressing in some way the infinite beauty of God in works made by human hands. Their dedication to the increase of God's praise and of his glory is more complete, the more exclusively they are devoted to turning men's minds devoutly toward God (*Sacrosanctum Concilium*, 122)" (2513). Truth is beautiful. The beautiful is true.

Truth works better than lies. Truth grounds the great and confident cultures and civilizations of history. Truth frees us. To belong to Jesus is to belong to truth.

Reflection

1. *What is the major lesson of the eighth commandment?*
   " 'You shall not bear false witness against your neighbor' (Ex 20:16). . . .
   "Truth or truthfulness is the virtue which consists in showing oneself true in deeds and truthful in words, and guarding against duplicity, dissimulation, and hypocrisy" (*Catechism*, 2504-2505).

2. *What are sins against this commandment?*
   Lies, calumny, slander, and false witness against another. A fault committed against the truth demands reparation. The sacramental secret is inviolable. (Professional secrets should be protected.) (cf. *Catechism*, 2506-2511)

3. *What about the truth in public forums?*
   "Society has a right to information based on truth, freedom, and justice. One should practice moderation and discipline in the use of the social communications media" (*Catechism*, 2512).

Prayer

Jesus, living truth, give me the gift of truth and the confidence that I can know both divine and human truth. Show me the unity of truth, love, and freedom.

Resource

Catechism, 2464-2513

Glossary

Relativism. Means that one cannot know objective truth. One can only know opinions.

Subjectivism. Similar to relativism. The subject is the individual person who relies on oneself alone as the source of right and wrong, true and false, good and bad. Also called individualism.

Truth. In the order of Revelation, the teachings of the Father in the Old Testament, the teachings of the Son in the Gospels, the teachings of the Holy Spirit in the Acts of the Apostles and the epistles. All these teachings are proposed by the Magisterium of the Church under the guidance of the Spirit. In the human order, truth is the objective expression of good/bad, true/false, and right/wrong by the light of reason.

Life Application

1. Someone has said that "lying is as American as apple pie." What do I think of this? What difficulties have I found with truth telling in my experience? What is the best way to teach children to tell the truth?

2. Many people get angry with the violation of "truth in advertising." How can producers be motivated to tell the truth in their ads? The media often give negative presentations about Catholics — some true, but often untruthful because the whole story is not told. What should be done about it?

3. How did I learn to tell the truth to my family, my employers, my friends, my confessor? How do I feel when I have been lied to? Why is honesty the best policy?

Focus

The words "image," "appearance," and "outwardly" are crucial to understanding the morality of the evil. While they seem to lack any motivation to be good, they intensely desire to appear good. Their "goodness" is all on a level of pretense. It is . . . a lie. This is why they are the "people of the lie."

Actually the lie is designed not so much to deceive others as to deceive themselves. They cannot or will not bear the pain of self-reproach. . . . Yet the self-deceit would be unnecessary if the evil had no sense of right and wrong. We lie only when we are attempting to cover up something we know to be illicit.

The essential component of evil is not the absence of a sense of sin or imperfection but the unwillingness to tolerate that sense. At one and the same time, [evil people] are aware of their evil and desperately trying to avoid the awareness. . . . [They sweep] the evidence of their evil under the rug of their consciousness. . . . We become evil by attempting to hide from ourselves. . . .

M. Scott Peck, *People of the Lie*

Chapter 52

The Ninth Commandment
– Cleanse Your Heart

The heart is the seat of moral personality.
Catechism, 2517

In the movie *Fatal Attraction*, lust ensnares a married man into a relationship with a beautiful, psychotic woman. The encounter nearly kills him. In the biblical book of Tobit, Sarah's seven husbands die on their wedding night. The virginal Sarah approached marriage with a pure heart. Her husbands came with lust. God pitied Sarah and sent her a chaste man, Tobit. They married and lived happily ever after.

The sixth commandment promotes fidelity. The ninth commandment upholds chastity. Both virtues strengthen the bond of marriage. People confuse celibacy with chastity. Celibates abstain from sex, but must also be chaste in their hearts. Spouses engage in sex with each other, but should also be chaste in their hearts.

Chastity of body for an unmarried person means abstinence from sex. For spouses it means no sex with anyone else.

Chastity of heart for both married and unmarried (celibates, singles, widows, widowers) deals with a good conscience, the intention to love others and not exploit them, the desire to do God's will. Scripture speaks here of the "clean of heart." Jesus says, "Blessed are the clean of heart, for they will see God" (Mt 5:8). Chastity of heart means rejecting lust.

When the biblical King David repented of his sins of adultery and murder, he begged God to clean his heart. Why? Because moral troubles in the body begin in the heart. In the story of "Chaste Susanna," Scripture contrasts her clean heart with the unclean hearts of the lustful elders.

Just as David prayed for purity of heart, so should we.

Lust undermines purity of heart. Purity restrains the passions. In lust the passions are out of control. Both the sixth and ninth commandments forbid lust and its outcomes: fornication, adultery, masturbation, pornography, prostitution, sexual abuse of others, indulgence in sexual fantasy.

Homosexual acts are also forbidden. At the same time, homosexual people should be treated with respect, compassion, and sensitivity (see *Catechism*, 2357-2359).

Two conflicting invitations challenge contemporary women and men.

The erotic society broadcasts its insistent messages about love without responsibility and sex without guilt. Jesus invites us to honor purity and to love chastely. Our permissive culture lies to its constituents, promising happiness through free love and irresponsible sex. Jesus really does deliver happiness through his message about real love and responsible sex.

God created our sexual nature for goodness and loveliness. Christ redeemed it for grace and gracefulness. The presence of grace in sex makes it "graceful." The absence of grace in sex makes it "disgraceful." Christ gave us the Sacrament of Marriage to make sexual love graceful.

The Church offers the compassion of Jesus for those committing sexual sins, making the forgiveness of God who is "rich in mercy" (Eph 2:4) available in the Sacrament of Reconciliation. The "clean of heart" really do experience genuine happiness.

Reflection

1. *What does the ninth commandment teach?*

"You shall not covet your neighbor's wife" (Deut 5:21).

" 'Everyone who looks at a woman lustfully has already committed adultery with her in his heart ' (Mt 5:28).

"The ninth commandment warns against lust or carnal concupiscence" (*Catechism*, 2528-2529).

2. *What should be our response to lust?*

"The struggle against carnal lust involves purifying the heart and practicing temperance.

"Purity of heart will enable us to see God: it enables us even now to see things according to God" (*Catechism*, 2530-2531).

3. *How do we purify our hearts?*

"Purification of the heart demands prayer, the practice of chastity, purity of intention and of vision.

"Purity of heart requires the modesty which is patience, decency, and discretion. Modesty protects the intimate center of the person" (*Catechism*, 2532-2533).

Prayer

A clean heart create for me, O God. / Cleanse me of sin . . . / that I may be purified; / wash me, and I shall be whiter than snow. . . . / Thoroughly wash me from my guilt / and of my sin cleanse me.

Ps 51:12, 9, 4

Resource
Catechism, 2514-2533

Glossary
Celibacy. Abstinence from sexual behavior. Priests in the Western Church and bishops in the Eastern Church take the vow of celibacy. So also do male members of religious orders and congregations. Female religious take the vow of virginity. Single people are expected to abstain from sex.

Chastity. Bodily chastity means abstaining from sex outside of marriage. For spouses it means no sex with anyone else. Chastity of heart means overcoming sexual lust for anyone, because lust degrades, dehumanizes, and exploits the other for one's selfish pleasure. Married and unmarried people (priestly and religious celibates, singles, widows, widowers) should have chastity of heart.

Life Application
1. Sex education can take two forms. First: "They are going to do it anyhow, so let's make it safe (free of disease) and responsible (no pregnancy)." Second: Abstinence from sex until marriage. It's a hundred percent effective. How can I make the case for abstinence, in opposition to the cultural tide today?
2. When young people are trained in the virtue of chastity, they will have a better chance of being chaste. What are five good ways to make this happen?
3. Misguided moral education leaves lust and sex up to the feelings and choices of the person. Why is this disastrous for happiness, marriage, and stability in our culture?

Focus
Is abstinence a realistic expectation? Yes and no. No, if the expectation is that all youngsters will wait until marriage before having sex. Yes, if it means that a majority can be persuaded that postponing sex is the right thing to do. It is true that some will "do it anyway. . . ." It is also true that actual behavior tends to fall below the cultural ideal. What this means in practice, however, is that the higher the cultural standard is set, the farther actual behavior rises to meet it. In turn, the lower . . . its standard, the farther below it actual behavior will sink.

. . . Once the standard falls to the level of recreational sex —about where it is now — we shouldn't be surprised to find that exploitative sex has become the norm for many or that date rape has become a major problem.

William Kilpatrick, *Why Johnny Can't Tell Right From Wrong*

Chapter 53

The Tenth Commandment – Reject Greed

The tenth commandment forbids greed and the desire to amass earthly goods without limit.

Catechism, 2536

Jesus once told a story about a greedy farmer. The man kept buying more land and increasing his harvests. He tore down his old barns and built bigger ones. He loved his possessions and dreamed of how happy they would make him. Then God said, "You fool. This night your life will be demanded of you." Jesus then delivered the moral of the story. "Thus will it be for the one who stores up treasure for himself but is not rich in what matters to God" (Lk 12:16-21).

The tenth commandment examines greed and its child, power. Nothing corrupts us more. "For the love of money is the root of all evils, and some people in their desire for it have strayed from the faith and have pierced themselves with many pains" (1 Tm 6:10).

Greedy people love money and the power it brings. But power corrupts, and absolute power corrupts absolutely.

Money alone does not pervert us. The "love of money" destroys us. When wealth becomes an end in itself and not a means to reasonable security and generosity to others, then it brutalizes us.

Greed (or covetousness and avarice) kills compassion for others. Greed hides behind disguises such as thrift, security, drive, the nature of business. There are two kinds of wealth, real and artificial. Real wealth is limited. How many beds can you sleep in? How many dresses or suits can you wear? Artificial wealth (stocks, bonds, credit) seems limitless. The love of artificial wealth causes a boundless craving.

How can we fight greed? Letting go of envy is one way. Developing a desire for God is a better way. The virtue of generosity drives out greed. The world has two kinds of people: givers and getters. Givers give. Getters take. Givers learn the secret of happiness. It is only in giving that we receive. Getters master the art of making others unhappy and securing misery for themselves.

What miracle is found in all four Gospels and twice in one of them? The multiplication of the loaves. The miracle foreshadows the Eucharist, in which we have the total wealth of the Church. The miracle also illustrates the multiplier effect of giving. The bread is multiplied in the giving.

"God loves a cheerful giver" (2 Cor 9:7). Greedy people create a culture of scarcity. The richer they get, the more homeless people walk the streets. Giving people create a culture of abundance. Their "Midas touch" is for the common good. Getters shrink the pie. Givers make a bigger pie.

Getters plunder the environment, kill the fish, burn the trees, and poison our arteries and lungs. Givers smell the roses, plant new trees, clean the streams, and make the air safe.

Givers value a simple lifestyle. They do not kill time. They take time to appreciate life. They are not addicted to speed. They slow down and contemplate the precious gifts of God's creation. Getters are immoral dinosaurs whose jaws eat the world. Givers are moral humans whose hands give a caring touch and make the world bigger than it seems to be.

Reflection

1. *What is the teaching of the tenth commandment?*
   "You shall not desire your neighbor's house, his field . . . or anything that is your neighbor's" (Deut 5:21).
   " 'Where your treasure is, there will your heart be also' (Mt 6:21)" (*Catechism*, 2551).

2. *How does envy cause greed?*
   "Envy is a sadness at the sight of another's goods and the immoderate desire to have them for oneself. It is a capital sin.
   "The baptized person combats envy through good-will, humility, and abandonment to the providence of God" (*Catechism*, 2553-2554).

3. *What is the biblical counterpoint to greed?*
   "Christ's faithful 'have crucified the flesh with its passions and desires' (Gal 5:24); they are led by the Spirit and follow his desires.
   "Detachment from riches is necessary for entering the Kingdom of heaven" (*Catechism*, 2555-2556).

Prayer

Lord, deliver me from greed and avarice. Fill me with your spirit of giving and generosity. Show me how to be a giver. Stop me from being a getter. Endow me with the best kind of "Midas touch," one that fills the world with the abundance of love, the gold of affection. Deliver me from the devil of envy and infuse in me the angel of giving.

Resource

Catechism, 2534-2557

Glossary

Covetousness. Another name for greed. Usually applies to a selfish and unrestrained desire and effort to acquire material wealth and the power that comes with it.

Love of Money. Money alone does not corrupt us. It is the "love of money" that generates envy and greed and its goal of power and domination.

Life Application

1. How happy am I with my way of life? What is my attitude toward money? Beyond security and the future of my children, what do I see money doing for me and my family? How much does envy (the old, "keeping up with the Joneses") play in my attitude to money?

2. Do I like to play power games? Where does prudent control phase into forms of tyranny in my dealings with others? In what way does power seeking enter into the goals I have set for myself? What am I doing to temper any desire to dominate others?

3. How attuned am I to environmental concerns? What conservation and recycling practices have I adopted? In what way have I contributed to public policy at the local, state, and national levels regarding the protection of the environment?

Focus

If human vices such as greed and envy are systematically cultivated, the inevitable result is nothing less than a collapse of intelligence. A man driven by greed loses the power of seeing things as they actually are, of seeing things in their roundness and wholeness, and his very successes become failures. If whole societies become infected by these vices, they may indeed achieve astonishing things, but they become increasingly incapable of solving the most elementary problems of everyday existence. . . .

I suggest that the foundations of peace cannot be laid by universal prosperity, in the modern sense, because such prosperity, if attainable at all, is attainable only by cultivating such drives as greed and envy, which destroy intelligence, happiness, serenity, and thereby, the peaceableness of man. It could well be that rich people treasure peace more highly than poor people, but only if they feel utterly secure — and this is a contradiction in terms. Their wealth depends on making inordinately large demands on limited world resources and thus puts them on an unavoidable collision course — not primarily with the poor (who are weak and defenseless) but with other rich people.

No one is really working for peace unless he is working primarily for the restoration of wisdom.

E. F. Schumacher, *Small Is Beautiful*

Part Four

Our Father: The Faith Prayed

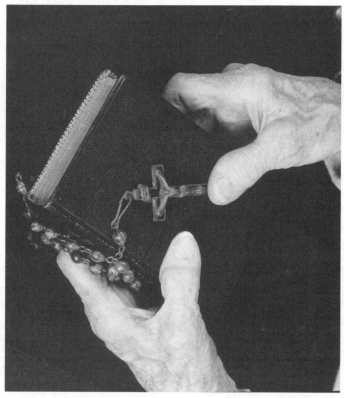

Chapter 54

Prayer Is the Power of the Heart

Christian prayer is a covenant relationship between God and man in Christ.
Catechism, 2564

An old woman tells a story of her being in the hospital and full of pain. She did not have the courage to take the tests that would reveal what was wrong. One morning a member of her parish visited her and told her that a group of her friends were forming a prayer circle for her. They planned to spend the whole night in prayer for her. That night she slept like a child. In the morning she felt strong enough to take the tests. She soon regained her health.

Dr. Alexis Carrell wrote, "Make a habit of sincere prayer. Then your life will be noticeably changed. Prayer is the world's most powerful form of energy."

The first three parts of the *Catechism* — Creed, Sacraments, Commandments — describe falling in love with God. The fourth part on Prayer deals with staying in love with God. Prayer provides the faith to believe, the fidelity to sacramental celebration, and the courage to live the commandments. Prayer is the driving force for living faith, lively liturgy, and fortitude in moral living.

The *Catechism* treats of prayer in two parts. The first section describes God's Revelation and gift of prayer. The second section meditates on the seven petitions of the Our Father.

The Bible would be unthinkable without prayer. The biblical history of salvation has thousands of references to prayer, from the sacrifices of Abel, Noah, Abraham, and Moses to the psalms of David to the canticles, hymns, and faith outpourings found in chapter after chapter.

The New Testament continues this preoccupation with prayer. Jesus teaches the apostles to pray and witnesses prayer by his nights spent in meditation. Pentecost happens after nine days of prayer. The apostles pray in all kinds of situations. In countless ways the Bible is a record of prayer as the energizing power of salvation history.

Scripture shows prayer happening in numerous forms: singing, dancing, talking, arms raised to heaven, hands with open palms, processions, silences, repeated short sayings, lengthy outpourings. There is prayer in solitude and in groups; prayer in a temple and prayer on a mountain; prayer in time of peace and also in war; prayer for begging favors, thanking for gifts, sheer adoration and tumultuous rejoicing in God. The first and last sayings of Christ's seven words from the Cross are prayers.

Revelation is an ocean of prayer. Hence the best training book for prayer is the Bible. It provides prayer forms and styles for every mood and need of the human heart. One of the most effective ways of making sense of the Bible is to pray. Why? Because prayer is the language of faith, and the Bible is a book of faith. That is why the Church's liturgical words are mostly taken from the Bible. Revelation comes alive in prayer.

"Pray without ceasing. In all circumstances give thanks, for this is the will of God for you in Christ Jesus" (1 Thes 5:17-18). Let this be in the form of hymns, words, silences, sighings, meditation, contemplation, centering prayer, psalms, worship, adoration, petition, thanksgiving. Get in touch with God. Love awaits you.

Reflection

1. *Who teaches prayer and what are its forms?*

   "The Holy Spirit who teaches the Church and recalls to her all that Jesus said also instructs her in the life of prayer, inspiring new expressions of the same basic forms of prayer: blessing, petition, intercession, thanksgiving, and praise" (*Catechism*, 2644).

2. *What settings are favorable to prayer?*

   "The most appropriate places for prayer are personal or family oratories, monasteries, places of pilgrimage, and above all the church, which is the proper place for liturgical prayer for the parish community and the privileged place for Eucharistic adoration" (*Catechism*, 2696).

3. *Where is the best setting for prayer education?*

   "The Christian family is the first place for education in prayer" (*Catechism*, 2694).

Prayer

Lord, teach me to pray. I do not know how to pray as I ought. Send your Spirit to lead me in prayer. Give me the humility and strength to walk a lifelong journey of prayer.

Resource

Catechism, 2558-2758

Glossary

Kinds of Prayer. Prayer mainly takes shape as (1) blessing and adoration, (2) petition, (3) intercession, (4) thanksgiving, and (5) praise. These attitudes of prayer permeate vocal prayer in its liturgical and devotional aspects — and silent prayer in its meditative and contemplative expressions.

Prayer

Prayer is the ascent of the mind to God or the request for suitable blessings from God. St. Thérèse of Lisieux says, "For me, prayer is a surge of the heart; it is a simple look turned toward heaven, it is a cry of recognition and of love, embracing both trial and joy" (*Catechism*, 2558). "Prayer is the raising of one's mind and heart to God or the requesting of good things from God" (St. John Damascene; *Catechism*, 2559).

Life Application

1. How attracted am I to prayer? How does my personal prayer affect my participation in liturgical prayer? How regularly do I pray? Is my prayer hard work, easy, or a bit of both? What am I doing to improve my prayer life? Why should I pray?
2. Have I discovered the value of daily meditation? How consistently is my meditation directed to Jesus leading me to the Father in the Spirit? What benefits have I derived from meditation? Have I found centering prayer a helpful form of meditation?
3. What books do I read to motivate me to prayer? Which saints appeal to me because of their devotion to prayer? What is the connection between prayer and my faith and my relationship to Jesus?

Focus

Prayer to *Jesus* is answered by him already during his ministry, through signs that anticipate the power of his death and Resurrection: Jesus hears the prayer of faith, expressed in words (the leper, Jairus, the Canaanite woman, the good thief) or in silence (the bearers of the paralytic, the woman with a hemorrhage who touches his clothes, the tears and ointment of the sinful woman). The urgent request of the blind men, "Have mercy on us, Son of David" . . . has been renewed in the traditional prayer to Jesus known as the *Jesus Prayer*: "Lord Jesus Christ, Son of God, have mercy on me, a sinner." Healing infirmities or forgiving sins, Jesus always responds to a prayer offered in faith: "Your faith has made you well; go in peace."

St. Augustine wonderfully summarizes the three dimensions of Jesus' prayer: "He prays for us as our priest, prays in us as our Head, and is prayed to by us as our God. Therefore let us acknowledge our voice in him and his in us."

Catechism, 2616

The Seven Lessons of the Our Father

The Lord's Prayer "is truly the summary of the whole gospel" (Tertullian).

Catechism, 2761

Christ's prayer life so impressed the apostles that they asked him, "Lord, teach us to pray" (Lk 11:1). Jesus responded by teaching them the Our Father.

Ever since, saints have outdone themselves extolling the perfection of this prayer and explaining it. St. Augustine wrote seven commentaries on it. St. Thomas Aquinas said, "The Lord's Prayer is the perfect prayer." St. Teresa of Ávila found the first two words so inexpressibly beautiful that she could hardly get beyond them. The Church never has a liturgy without praying the Our Father. The Son of God has taught us the words to pray to God. It contains the essence of the Gospel.

The prayer starts with "Our." We never pray alone. In the solidarity of the Body of Christ, hundreds of millions of Catholics pray with us. Then we say, "Father." Jesus tells us to call God our "Father." This means both comfort and challenge. A father is easy to please but hard to satisfy. God our Father loves us and demands much of us. We pray for what we need to respond to the challenge and experience salvation.

The Our Father contains seven petitions. The first three deal with God. The last four concern us. Each petition is a lesson in praying.

1. *Hallowed be thy name.* This teaches us to reverence God's holiness. God is totally other than ourselves. God is mystery. God is love. We learn never to domesticate God and exploit him for our own purposes. That would be idolatry.

2. *Thy kingdom come.* Jesus brought us the kingdom, which is salvation from sin and eternal life. The kingdom here results in love, mercy, and justice. Hereafter, the kingdom is absolute joy. The kingdom is available, but we cannot have it unless we pray for it.

3. *Thy will be done.* Jesus rarely boasted except to say he always did the Father's will. Pride says, "I do my thing." Humility says, "I do God's will." We must pray for this because God's will is both difficult to discern and hard to practice. Ask the Holy Spirit for the gifts of knowledge and courage.

4. *Give us this day our daily bread.* All physical and spiritual nourishment comes ultimately from God. Our Father is the creative and productive presence behind all food — the bread of the table and the bread of the altar.

We ought to pray every day for both. This helps us see Our Father as life-giver.

5. *Forgive us our trespasses.* Only our Father can forgive our sins. His fatherly forgiveness is a model for our forgiving others. If we do not forgive others, God will not forgive us.

6. *Lead us not into temptation.* In a world of freedom, temptation will happen. We pray that God will help us avoid temptation and fight against it when it happens. We face a moral struggle every day. We need divine power to prevail against sin.

7. *But deliver us from evil.* Our Father's plan of salvation was accomplished in Jesus Christ. We should pray always that this redemption be effective in our lives.

In the Eucharistic celebration we conclude the Our Father with a doxology, "For the kingdom, the power, and the glory are yours, now and for ever." This says it all. The praise of God sums up Christian life and Catholic religion. Glory be to God!

Reflection

1. *Why is the Our Father so important?*

" 'The Lord's Prayer is truly the summary of the whole gospel' (Tertullian), the 'most perfect of prayers' (St. Thomas Aquinas). It is at the center of the Scriptures.

"It is called 'the Lord's Prayer' because it comes to us from the Lord Jesus, the master and model of our prayer" (*Catechism*, 2774-2775).

2. *How can we call God our "Father"?*

". . . because the Son of God made man has revealed him to us. In this Son, through Baptism, we are incorporated and adopted as sons of God" (*Catechism*, 2798).

3. *Why do we say "Our" Father?*

"When we say 'Our' Father, we are invoking the new covenant in Jesus Christ, communion with the Holy Trinity, and the divine love which spreads through the Church to encompass the world" (*Catechism*, 2801).

Prayer

Our Father who art in heaven, hallowed be thy name. Thy kingdom come. Thy will be done on earth, as it is in heaven. Give us this day our daily bread, and forgive us our trespasses, as we forgive those who trespass against us, and lead us not into temptation, but deliver us from evil. Amen.

Resource

Catechism, 2759-2865

Glossary

Hallowed. Old English word for holy. In the Our Father we sound like we are saying that God's name should become holy. But God and his name are already holy. Our petition is to remind us of God's holiness.

Trespasses. These are sins. We ask forgiveness for our sins to the extent that we have forgiven others their sins against us.

Life Application

1. As I review the seven petitions of the Our Father, how do I realize they contain all the aspects of what it means to pray? Which of the seven petitions apply most especially to my life and therefore my need to pray that petition more vigorously?
2. Why did Jesus teach us to say *Our* Father instead of *My* Father? What is the basic difference between my relationship to the Father and my relationship to Jesus?
3. When I say the word *kingdom,* what associations come to my mind in the context of the Our Father? What is the connection between Christ's kingdom and salvation? How strongly do we mean, "Thy will be done?"

Focus

Let us always desire the happy life from the Lord God and always pray for it. [This is why] we turn our mind to . . . prayer at appointed hours, since that desire grows lukewarm . . . from our involvement in other concerns and occupations. We remind ourselves through the words of prayer to focus our attention on the object of our desire; otherwise, the desire . . . may be totally extinguished unless it is repeatedly stirred into flame. . . .

The monks in Egypt are said to offer frequent prayers, but these are very short and hurled like swift javelins. Otherwise their watchful attention . . . could be dulled. . . .

To spend much time in prayer is to knock with a persistent and holy fervor at the door of the one whom we beseech. This task is generally accomplished more through sighs than words, more through weeping than speech. [God] places our tears in his sight, and our sighs are not hidden from him, for he has established all things through his Word and does not seek human words.

St. Augustine

Bibliography

Church Documents

Catechism of the Catholic Church, Congregation for the Doctrine of the Faith (Washington, D.C.: United States Catholic Conference, 1994, 1997).

Educational Guidance in Human Love, Outlines for Sex Education (Rome: Sacred Congregation for Catholic Education, 1983).

General Catechetical Directory, Congregation for the Clergy (Washington, D.C.: United States Catholic Conference, 1971).

John Paul II, Pope, *Catechesi Tradendae*, Apostolic Exhortation on Instruction and Formation in the Faith (Washington, D.C. United States Catholic Conference, 1979).

John Paul II, Pope, *Redemptoris Missio* ("The Mission of the Redeemer"), Encyclical on Evangelization (Washington, D.C.: United States Catholic Conference, 1991).

John Paul II, Pope, *Veritatis Splendor*, Encyclical on Catholic Moral Teaching (Washington, D.C.: United States Catholic Conference, 1993).

Paul VI, Pope, *Evangelii Nuntiandi*, Apostolic Exhortation on Evangelization (Washington, D.C.: United States Catholic Conference, 1975).

Religious Dimension of Education in a Catholic School, The (Rome: Congregation for Catholic Education, 1988).

Sharing the Light of Faith, (Washington, D.C.: United States Catholic Conference, 1979).

Vatican Council II: The Conciliar and Post Conciliar Documents, New Revised Edition (Northport, N.Y.: Costello Publishing Company, Inc., 1992).

Other Resources

Adult Catechesis in the Christian Community, International Council for Catechesis (Washington, D.C.: NCEA Publications, 1990).

Alexander, A.L. (ed.), *Poems That Touch the Heart* (New York: Doubleday, 1956).

Augustine, St., *Confessions* (New York: Viking Penguin, 1961).

Balthasar, Hans Urs von, *Mary for Today* (San Francisco: Ignatius Press, 1988).

Covey, Stephen R., *The 7 Habits of Highly Effective People* (New York: Simon and Schuster, 1989).

Daughters of St. Paul, *John Paul II in America* (Boston: St. Paul Books and Media, 1987).

De Lubac, Henri, S.J., *The Splendor of the Church* (San Francisco: Ignatius Press, 1986).

Gallup, George, Jr., and Jim Castelli, *The People's Religion* (New York: Macmillan, 1989).

Hebblethwaite, Peter, *Pope John XXIII* (New York: Doubleday, 1985).

Hirsch, E.D., *Cultural Literacy*, (Houghton Mifflin, 1987). (Contains useful arguments that could be applied to the quest for religious literacy).

Kelly, Msgr. Francis D., *The Mystery We Proclaim* (Huntington, Ind.: Our Sunday Visitor, 1993). (Excellent brief history of the modern catechetical movement, introduction to the new *Catechism*, and lastly, an ecclesial method for catechesis.)

Ker, Ian, *Newman: On Being a Christian* (London: HarperCollins, 1990).

Kilpatrick, William, *Why Johnny Can't Tell Right From Wrong* (New York: Simon and Schuster, 1992). (A powerful critique of the popular, but failed, methods of teaching morality in schools. The author gives a positive plan for virtue education and how to do it.)

Kreeft, Peter, *Fundamentals of the Faith* (San Francisco: Ignatius Press, 1988).

Lewis, C.S., *Mere Christianity* (New York: Macmillan, 1952).

Liturgy of the Hours, The, Vol. I-IV (New York: Catholic Book Publishing Co., 1976; English translation by the International Commission on English in the Liturgy, Inc., 1975. All rights reserved).

Marmion, Abbot Columba, O.S.B., *Christ the Life of the Soul* (St. Louis: Herder, 1926).

Newman, John Henry Cardinal, *Parochial and Plain Sermons* (San Francisco: Ignatius Press, 1987).

Newsweek, "Talking to God," January 6, 1992, Kenneth L. Woodward, et al.

_____,"A Time to Seek," December 17, 1990, Kenneth L. Woodward, et al.

O'Brien, Rev. John A., *The Faith of Millions* (Huntington, Ind.: Our Sunday Visitor, 1974).

O'Connor, Edward D., *The Catholic Vision* (Huntington, Ind.: Our Sunday Visitor, 1992). (This book would serve as a superb text on Catholicism for college-level students.)

Peck, M. Scott, *People of the Lie: The Hope for Healing Human Evil* (New York: Simon and Schuster, 1985).

Phillips, J.B., *Your God Is Too Small* (New York: Macmillan, 1964).

Rahner, Karl, *Mary, Mother of the Lord* (St. Louis: Herder, date n.a.).

Schumacher, E.F., *Small Is Beautiful: Economics as if People Mattered* (New York: HarperCollins, 1989).

Sheed, Frank, and Maisie Ward, *Catholic Evidence Training Outlines* (Ann Arbor, Mich.: Catholic Evidence Guild, 1992).

Sheen, Archbishop Fulton J., *Life of Christ* (New York: Image, 1970).

_____, *Three to Get Married* (London: Blandon Press, 1953).

Thornton, Martin, *English Spirituality* (Cambridge: Cowley Publications, 1986).

Time, "A Pencil in the Hand of God," December 4, 1989, Edward W. Desmond.

Tolstoy, Leo, *Where Love Is, There Is God Also* (Brookings, Ore.: Sandpiper, 1987).

Wuerl, Bishop Donald W., Ronald Lawler, O.F.M. Cap., and Thomas Comerford Lawler, *The Teaching of Christ,* Fourth Edition (Huntington, Ind.: Our Sunday Visitor, 1995). (A widely praised catechism used in parishes, adult-education programs, RCIA, and convert classes.)

Young, Marjorie, and Adam Bujak, *Journeys to Glory* (New York: HarperCollins, 1976).

Appendices

PRAYERS EVERY CATHOLIC SHOULD KNOW

The Sign of the Cross
In the name of the Father, and of the Son, and of the Holy Spirit. Amen.

Our Father (Lord's Prayer)
Our Father who art in heaven, hallowed be thy name. Thy kingdom come. Thy will be done on earth, as it is in heaven. Give us this day our daily bread, and forgive us our trespasses, as we forgive those who trespass against us, and lead us not into temptation, but deliver us from evil. (For the kingdom, the power, and the glory are yours, now and for ever.) Amen.

Hail Mary
Hail Mary, full of grace, the Lord is with thee. Blessed art thou among women, and blessed is the fruit of thy womb, Jesus. Holy Mary, Mother of God, pray for us sinners now and at the hour of our death. Amen.

Prayer of Praise
Glory be to the Father, and to the Son, and to the Holy Spirit. As it was in the beginning, is now, and ever shall be, world without end. Amen.

Prayer to the Holy Spirit
Come Holy Spirit, fill the hearts of your faithful, and enkindle in us the fire of your divine love. Send forth your Spirit and we shall be created, and you shall renew the face of the earth.

O God, who instructed the hearts of the faithful by the light of your divine Spirit, grant us by that same Spirit to be truly wise and to rejoice in your holy consolation. Through the same Christ our Lord. Amen.

Act of Contrition
O my God, I am heartily sorry for having offended thee, and I detest all my sins because of thy just punishments. But most of all because they offend thee, my God, who art all good and deserving of all my love. I firmly resolve, with the help of thy grace, to confess my sins, to do penance, and to amend my life. Amen.

Apostles' Creed

I believe in God, the Father almighty, creator of heaven and earth, and in Jesus Christ, his only Son, our Lord, who was conceived by the Holy Spirit, born of the Virgin Mary, suffered under Pontius Pilate, was crucified, died, and was buried. He descended into hell. The third day he arose again from the dead. He ascended into heaven and is seated at the right hand of God the Father almighty. From thence, he shall come again to judge the living and the dead. I believe in the Holy Spirit, the holy Catholic Church, the communion of saints, the forgiveness of sins, the resurrection of the body, and life everlasting. Amen.

Act of Faith

O my God, I firmly believe that you are one God in three divine persons, Father, Son, and Holy Spirit; I believe that your Divine Son became man and died for our sins, and that he will come to judge the living and the dead. I believe these and all the truths which the holy Catholic Church teaches, because you revealed them, who can neither deceive nor be deceived. Amen.

Act of Hope

O my God, relying on your infinite goodness and promises, I hope to obtain pardon of my sins, the help of your grace, and life everlasting, through the merits of Jesus Christ, my Lord and Redeemer. Amen.

Act of Love

O my God, I love you above all things, with my whole heart and soul, because you are all good and worthy of all love. I love my neighbor as myself for the love of you. I forgive all who have injured me, and I ask pardon of all whom I have injured. Amen.

THE ROSARY

The Rosary is an important prayer in Catholic tradition. It involves vocal prayers (Apostles' Creed, Our Father, Hail Mary, Prayer of Praise), meditative prayer (on the mysteries of the Rosary), and usually the use of rosary beads as a person or a group of people say the rosary.

Joyful Mysteries –
events surrounding the birth and early life of Jesus

    Annunciation to Mary
    Visitation of Mary to Elizabeth
    Birth of Jesus
    Presentation in the Temple
    Finding the Child Jesus in the Temple

Sorrowful Mysteries –
events surrounding the Passion and death of Jesus

    Agony in the Garden
    Scourging at the Pillar
    Crowning with Thorns
    Jesus Carries His Cross
    Death of Jesus on the Cross

Glorious Mysteries –
events and faith of the early Church's experience

    Resurrection of Jesus from the Tomb
    Ascension into Heaven
    Descent of the Holy Spirit upon the Apostles
    Assumption of Mary into Heaven
    Coronation of Mary as Queen of Heaven and Earth

SEVEN SACRAMENTS IN THE CATHOLIC CHURCH

Baptism
Confirmation
Eucharist (Communion)
Reconciliation (Penance, Confession)
Marriage
Orders (formerly called Holy Orders)
Anointing of the Sick (formerly called Extreme Unction)

SEVEN CAPITAL SINS

Pride
Covetousness
Lust
Anger
Gluttony
Envy
Sloth

ORDER OF THE MASS

Gathering and Entrance Procession

Greeting
Opening Prayer
Prayer of Praise
Penitential Rite

Liturgy of the Word

First Reading (usually from the Old Testament)
Psalm Response
Second Reading (usually from an epistle in the New Testament)
Gospel
Homily
Creed
Prayer of the Faithful

Liturgy of the Eucharist

Preparation and Offering of the Gifts of Bread and Wine
Preface Prayer of Praise and Thanksgiving
Eucharistic Prayer (including words of consecration and concluding
    with the community's great Amen)
Communion Rite: Lord's Prayer, Sign of Peace, Communion,
    Meditation
Concluding Prayer
Blessing
Dismissal

RITE OF RECONCILIATION FOR INDIVIDUALS
(PENANCE, CONFESSION)

Greeting from the Priest

Sign of the Cross

Scripture Passage

Confession of Sins

> (Here, honestly confess the sins that have been part of your life.
> All serious matter should be included, as well as less serious
> things that are troublesome in your life with the Lord.)

Advice and Spiritual Counseling

Penance

> (The prayer or good work that you will be asked to take on is a sign
> of your sincere repentance.)

Prayer of Sorrow or Contrition

Absolution: The Priest places his hands on your head (or extends his
right hand toward you) and prays these words of forgiveness:
"God, the Father of mercies, through the death and resurrection of his Son has reconciled the world to himself and sent the
Holy Spirit among us for the forgiveness of sins; through the
ministry of the Church may God give you pardon and peace,
and I absolve you from your sins in the name of the Father, and
of the Son, and of the Holy Spirit."

Prayer of Praise, such as:

Priest: "Give thanks to the Lord, for he is good."

Response: "His mercy endures forever."

Dismissal, such as:

"The Lord has freed you from your sins. Go in peace."

The Great Commandment

"You shall love the Lord your God with all your heart, with all your soul, and with all your mind. You shall love your neighbor as yourself" (Mt 22:37-39).

The Ten Commandments

(cf. Ex 20)

1. I am the Lord, your God. You shall honor no other god but me.
2. You shall not misuse the name of the Lord, your God.
3. You shall keep holy the Sabbath.
4. You shall honor your father and mother.
5. You shall not kill.
6. You shall not commit adultery.
7. You shall not steal.
8. You shall not bear false witness against your neighbor.
9. You shall not covet your neighbor's wife.
10. You shall not covet your neighbor's goods.

The Beatitudes

(cf. Mt 5)

1. Blessed are the poor in spirit; the reign of God is theirs.
2. Blessed are the sorrowing; they shall be consoled.
3. Blessed are the lowly; they shall inherit the land.
4. Blessed are they who hunger and thirst for holiness; they shall have their fill.
5. Blessed are they who show mercy; mercy shall be theirs.
6. Blessed are the single-hearted; they shall see God.
7. Blessed are the peacemakers; they shall be called sons of God.
8. Blessed are those persecuted for holiness sake; the reign of God is theirs.

Spiritual Works of Mercy

To admonish the sinner
To instruct the ignorant
To counsel the doubtful
To comfort the sorrowful
To bear wrongs patiently
To forgive all injuries
To pray for the living and the dead

Corporal Works of Mercy
> To feed the hungry
> To give drink to the thirsty
> To clothe the naked
> To visit the imprisoned
> To shelter the homeless
> To visit the sick
> To bury the dead

LAWS OF THE CHURCH

(The following is taken directly from the *Catechism*, 2041-2043.)

The precepts of the Church are set in the context of a moral life bound to and nourished by liturgical life. The obligatory character of these positive laws decreed by the pastoral authorities is meant to guarantee to the faithful the very necessary minimum in the spirit of prayer and moral effort, in the growth in love of God and neighbor:

The first precept ("You shall attend Mass on Sundays and holy days of obligation and rest from servile labor") requires the faithful to sanctify the day commemorating the Resurrection of the Lord as well as the principle liturgical feasts honoring the mysteries of the Lord, the Blessed Virgin Mary, and the saints; in the first place, by participating in the Eucharistic celebration, in which the Christian community is gathered, and by resting from those works and activities which could impede such a sanctification of these days.

The second precept ("You shall confess your sins at least once a year") ensures preparation for the Eucharist by the reception of the sacrament of reconciliation, which continues Baptism's work of conversion and forgiveness.

The third precept ("You shall receive the sacrament of the Eucharist at least during the Easter season") guarantees as a minimum the reception of the Lord's Body and Blood in connection with the Paschal feasts, the origin and center of the Christian liturgy.

The fourth precept ("You shall observe the days of fasting and abstinence established by the Church") ensures the times of ascesis and penance which prepare us for the liturgical feasts and help us acquire mastery over our instincts and freedom of heart.

The fifth precept ("You shall help to provide for the needs of the Church") means that the faithful are obliged to assist with the material needs of the Church, each according to his own ability.

HOLY DAYS OF OBLIGATION
(IN THE UNITED STATES)

January 1 — Solemnity of the Blessed Virgin Mary, the Mother of God

Ascension of the Lord (forty days after Easter)

August 15 — Assumption of the Blessed Virgin Mary

November 1 — All Saints

December 8 — Immaculate Conception of the Blessed Virgin Mary

December 25 — Christmas

(The precept to attend Mass is abrogated in the United States whenever the Solemnity of the Blessed Virgin Mary, the Assumption, or All Saints falls on a Saturday or Monday. In most of the U.S. ecclesiastical provinces, the Ascension is transferred from Thursday to the following Sunday.)

REGULATIONS FOR FAST AND ABSTINENCE
(IN THE UNITED STATES)

Fasting means giving up food, or some kinds of food, for a specified period of time. In Church regulations, abstinence means giving up meat for certain times. (For many years, abstinence was required of Catholics every Friday, as a communal way of observing Friday as a day for special penance. Catholics are no longer required to abstain from meat each Friday, although they are expected to exercise some form of penance on that day, in remembrance of Jesus' death for us.) Catholics are expected to fast from food and liquids (other than water and medicine) for one hour before receiving Holy Communion.

Certain days are also set aside as days of fast and abstinence for Catholics, when adults are expected to eat only minimum amounts of food, no meat, and nothing between meals at all. In the United States, Ash Wednesday and Good Friday are such days of fast and abstinence.

Index

About the Author

Father Alfred McBride, O.Praem., has been a leader in the field of religious education for more than three decades. To help implement the *Catechism of the Catholic Church*, he has written four books that make its teachings available to teens, adults, families, and college students, published by Our Sunday Visitor. He was executive director of religious education at the National Catholic Educational Association and has produced numerous catechetical writings including a multivolume Bible-study series published by Our Sunday Visitor. He presently teaches theology at Blessed John XXIII Seminary in Weston, Massachusetts.

Our Sunday Visitor . . .
Your Source for Discovering
the Riches of the Catholic Faith

Our Sunday Visitor has an extensive line of materials for young children, teens, and adults. Our books, Bibles, booklets, CD-ROMs, audios, and videos are available in bookstores worldwide.

To receive a FREE full-line catalog or for more information, call **Our Sunday Visitor** at **1-800-348-2440**. Or write, **Our Sunday Visitor** / 200 Noll Plaza / Huntington, IN 46750.

- -

Please send me: __A catalog
Please send me materials on:
__Apologetics and catechetics __Reference works
__Prayer books   __Heritage and the saints
__The family   __The parish

Name_____
Address_____Apt._____
City_____State_____Zip_____
Telephone (   ) _____
                                                    A29BBABP

- -

Please send a friend: __A catalog
Please send a friend materials on:
__Apologetics and catechetics __Reference works
__Prayer books   __Heritage and the saints
__The family   __The parish

Name_____
Address_____Apt._____
City_____State_____Zip_____
Telephone (   ) _____
                                                    A29BBABP

- -

Our Sunday Visitor
200 Noll Plaza
Huntington, IN 46750
Toll free: **1-800-348-2440**
E-mail: osvbooks@osv.com
Website: www.osv.com